NANCY RUSHED BACK, AND TO THE ASTONISHMENT OF
THE CLERK, SNATCHED UP HIS PRIVATE TELEPHONE.

The Bungalow Mystery.   *Page* 157

AS QUIETLY AS POSSIBLE SHE CLIMBED THE TRELLIS.
The Bungalow Mystery.   *Page* 96

LITTLE BY LITTLE THEY SUCCEEDED IN MOVING THE
TREE A SHORT WAY.

The Bungalow Mystery.   *Page* 59

SHE STEPPED OUT INTO WATER WHICH REACHED
NEARLY TO HER KNEES.

The Bungalow Mystery *Frontispiece (Page* 20)

NANCY DREW MYSTERY STORIES

THE BUNGALOW MYSTERY

By
CAROLYN KEENE

AUTHOR OF
NANCY DREW MYSTERY STORIES: THE SECRET OF THE OLD CLOCK
NANCY DREW MYSTERY STORIES: THE HIDDEN STAIRCASE

ILLUSTRATED BY
RUSSELL H. TANDY

WITH AN INTRODUCTION BY
P.M. CARLSON

FACSIMILE EDITION

1991
BEDFORD, MA
APPLEWOOD BOOKS
Distributed by The Globe Pequot Press
Chester, CT

For further information about these editions please write:
Applewood Books, 18 North Road, Bedford, MA 01730.

LIBRARY OF CONGRESS CATALOGING-IN-PUBLICATION DATA
Keene, Carolyn.
      The bungalow mystery / by Carolyn Keene;
illustrated by Russell H. Tandy; with an introduction by
P.M. Carlson.—Facsimile ed.
            p.   cm. — (Nancy Drew mystery stories)
      Summary: While trying to help a friend out of a
difficulty, teenage detective Nancy Drew has a perilous
experience in and around a deserted bungalow.
      ISBN 1-55709-157-9 : $12.95
      [1. Mystery and detective stories.]   I. Tandy,
Russell H., ill.   II. Title.   III. Series: Keene, Carolyn.
Nancy Drew mystery stories.
PZ7.K23Bt   1992   91-46732
[Fic]—dc20   CIP
                                                        AC

10 9 8 7 6 5 4 3 2

PUBLISHER'S NOTE

Applewood Books is pleased to reissue the original Hardy Boys and Nancy Drew books, just as they were originally published—the Hardy Boys in 1927 and Nancy Drew in 1930. In 1959, the books were condensed and rewritten, and since then, the original editions have been out of print.

Much has changed in America since the books were first issued. The modern reader may be delighted with the warmth and exactness of the language, the wholesome innocence of the characters, their engagement with the natural world, or the nonstop action without the use of violence; but just as well, the modern reader may be extremely uncomfortable with the racial and social stereotyping, the roles women play in these books, or the use of phrases or situations which may conjure up some response in the modern reader that was not felt by the reader of the times.

For good or bad, we Americans have changed quite a bit since these books were first issued. Many readers will remember these editions with great affection and will be delighted with their return; others will wonder why we just don't let them disappear. These books are part of our heritage. They are a window on our real past. For that reason, except for the addition of this note and the introduction by P.M. Carlson, we are presenting *The Bungalow Mystery* unedited and unchanged from its first edition.

Applewood Books
September 1991

NANCY AND ME

By

P.M. CARLSON

AUTHOR OF
THE MAGGIE RYAN MYSTERY SERIES: MURDER IN THE DOG DAYS
THE MAGGIE RYAN MYSTERY SERIES: MURDER MISREAD
THE MAGGIE RYAN MYSTERY SERIES: BAD BLOOD
& OTHERS

IN 1920 American women got the vote.

Less than a decade later, Nancy Drew was on the scene, beginning her immensely popular series of adventures. Young Nancy was the ideal modern woman-to-be: friendly, curious, loyal, and competent in a wide variety of skills. She was bright, of course, but she was also expert in swimming, running motorboats, calming distraught victims, escaping traps, even daredevil driving as she zipped her blue roadster from adventure to adventure. How I coveted that blue roadster! We readers were treated to exciting stories in which Nancy's brains and courage unraveled puzzles, exposed crooks, and restored her world to sunlit order once again. And these feats were accomplished by Nancy herself. True, she might ask a chum to come along sometimes. Her benevolent father, Carson Drew, was often useful for advice or backup. An admiring police force eventually took charge of the miscreants she caught. But in the end it was Nancy who solved the puzzles and collared the crooks.

Another important aspect of Nancy Drew's character was that despite her youth, she loved her work and took it seriously. She was an amateur only in the sense that she did not take money for her efforts. Her commitment to seeing cases through to the end and her pleasure in exercising her talents are the marks of a top professional. Nancy was no damsel in distress involved in adventures as the passive victim of an active evildoer, reacting rather than acting. She was active, too, hunting down criminals and facing them bravely.

The real world teems with situations full of crime and confusion and seemingly nice people with obscure motives. One reason we love mysteries is that they present us with just such situations, then lead us to the truth about them and, often, to just resolutions of the problems. The real world is seldom so obliging. Real-world truth and justice are elusive and partial. Yet we must confront crime and confusion all the same. Mysteries give us a chance to see how people might react to evil, how they cut through confusion, how they hold to ideals of truth and justice when the world goes bad. "Just entertainment," some say. But what makes mysteries so entertaining? In part, they grip us because they deal with issues that are important and universal: Evil. Truth. Justice. Courage.

For those of us who are female, of course, Nancy Drew has added importance. Growing up, we saw a society in which men were expected to run the nation and the economy and women were expected to run families and neighborhoods. In this constricted area we weren't expected to worry about the big questions of crime and evil, truth and justice. As we chafed under these limited expectations, it was a delight to encounter Nancy Drew with her subversive message: Yes, we're female, but we too can hunt down truth! We can fight for justice! We can have adventures! We can do it!

As I grew older, Nancy went underground in my mind, but she didn't abandon me. She was one of the influences that enabled me to aim for an advanced degree in the logical realm of science and statistics; and when I had time to read, I turned again to mysteries. Of course I loved the brilliance of Sayers's characters, the high spirits of Allingham's, the classic puzzles of Christie, the suspense in Chandler. But except for Miss Marple, who came to her answers by analogies rather than by logic and courage, the detective heroes were men. Like most women, I learned to identify with the heroes. Men and women alike long to solve problems and to make the world a better place, and if the character striving for these results was male, okay, I'd identify with him. I certainly didn't want to identify with some wimpy woman who needed rescuing. After all, I'd read Nancy Drew, and I still heard her whisper: We can do it!

When I decided to try writing a mystery series of my own, my first problem was to create a detective. The classical amateur detectives have been rather unlikely folks: a cocaine addict who wears deerstalker hats, a fat man who raises orchids and never leaves his brownstone, a nosy old woman in an English village. But by the time I started writing I'd raised two boys while teaching experimental psychology at the college level, and I knew from my own experience that the least likely detective of all was a working mother of toddlers. So Maggie Ryan was born: a hard-working statistician and a hard-working mom, who solved a murder from time to time.

I soon learned that there are a couple of good reasons that working mothers don't often become detectives. First, working moms have no time to spare. Juggling career, children, and marriage is asking a lot of any woman, even without adding sleuthing. Obviously, a working mother who would take time out to solve crimes had to be a special kind of person. Maggie would be very different from Nancy Drew, I thought. For instance, Maggie attended college, unlike Nancy, who never seemed to go to school at all. Maggie didn't stay the same age, like the perennially youthful Nancy. Maggie went on to get a job as a professional statistician, marry, have children, and enthusiastically combine her roles with that of sleuth. And of course Maggie's stories are set in the sixties and seventies, unlike the Nancy Drew I remembered, who lived in the thirties and forties. The people Maggie befriends include war survivors, rape victims, battered wives, abused children, old people who fear eviction. Finally, Nancy was single-minded about her detecting; Maggie's enthusiasms are broader. She understands the hurt the world can bring but remains high-spirited, irreverent, devoted to family and job and music and fun. Obviously, she has little in common with Nancy Drew.

Or does she? In retrospect, the debt to Nancy seems clear. I may have begun with the idea of a character who would grow into a mother willing to do some detecting on the side, but I ended with a woman who was lively, curious, athletic, loyal to her friends, and eager to help make a better world. Sound familiar? And even though she doesn't have a blue roadster, Maggie is very fond of her fast car.

I like to think the similarity goes deeper. There's a second reason mothers seldom appear as detectives. It has to do with society's mythologies. Good mothers are supposed to be selfless, living through their children with no lives of their own. But not surprisingly, mothers who try to live up to these expectations are seen as a drag, smothering their children's independence. Look at Nancy Drew herself; she has a kindly, distant father as mentor, Hannah to keep house, but no "good mother" around, trying to teach her that society thinks young women should stay on the sidelines. Even though Nancy broke down walls that said females shouldn't fight crime or have adventures, she left intact the ones that say motherhood rules out other activities. Of course it's true that most of us mothers are willing to make sacrifices for our families and are deeply involved in the activities of our husbands and children, but there's much more in our lives than that. So I feel that Maggie stands firmly in the subversive tradition of Nancy Drew when her stories say: Yes, we are loving, committed moms, but we too can hunt down truth! We can fight for justice! We can have adventures! We can do it!

I've discussed my own detective, my own debts to Nancy Drew. There are many of us writing mysteries today. We are very different people with very different stories to tell, and our books are a celebration of the many ways women can live their lives today. There are women detectives in light-hearted books by Elizabeth Peters, Carolyn Hart, Sharyn McCrumb, or Joan Hess, and tough women private eyes in darker stories from Sara Paretsky, Sue Grafton, Sandra Scoppettone, Linda Barnes, or Meg O'Brien. Businesswomen solve crimes in novels by Annette Meyers, Linda Grant, or Nancy Pickard; women cops solve them in books by Julie Smith, Margaret Maron, Susan Dunlap, and Lee Martin; women lawyers in Lia Matera, women professors in Amanda Cross. But I sense the spirit of courageous young truth-seeker Nancy Drew moving in them all.

Back in World War II, previously sheltered women stepped competently into the jobs vacated by soldiers. They ran factories, flew planes, built buildings, and did all kinds of things women weren't expected to do. Some people comment with astonishment on the splendid achievement of those women, but I'm not surprised. My theory is that Rosie the Riveter read Nancy Drew.

We can do it!

NANCY DREW MYSTERY STORIES

THE
BUNGALOW MYSTERY

BY

CAROLYN KEENE

AUTHOR OF
"THE SECRET OF THE OLD CLOCK,"
"THE HIDDEN STAIRCASE," ETC.

ILLUSTRATED BY

RUSSELL H. TANDY

NEW YORK
GROSSET & DUNLAP
PUBLISHERS

Made in the United States of America

NANCY DREW
MYSTERY STORIES

By CAROLYN KEENE

12mo. Cloth. Illustrated.

———

THE SECRET OF THE OLD CLOCK

THE HIDDEN STAIRCASE

THE BUNGALOW MYSTERY

(Other volumes in preparation)

———

GROSSET & DUNLAP, PUBLISHERS, NEW YORK

CONTENTS

iv   Contents

THE BUNGALOW
MYSTERY

CHAPTER 1

RACING THE STORM

"DON'T you think we should turn back,
Helen? It's getting dreadfully dark out here
on the lake and I don't like the look of those
big black clouds."

As Nancy Drew addressed her chum, Helen
Corning, she gazed anxiously up at the sky and
then out across a long expanse of water to the
distant shore.

The two girls were spending several days
at a camp located on Moon Lake, and on this
particular afternoon they had slipped away
for a delightful motorboat outing. They had
cruised aimlessly about for several hours, enjoying the lake scenery and, particularly, a
cool, refreshing breeze which brought them relief from an unseasonably torrid day, for it
was early summer.

1

Now, as Nancy studied the sky for the first time, she was alarmed to notice that it had become overcast.

"Helen, I'm afraid there's going to be a storm," she announced. "They come up so quickly on Moon Lake."

"You're right," Helen agreed uneasily. "It does look threatening. I didn't realize we were so far from shore. We'd better get back to camp as fast as we can."

"I guess we were having too good a time to notice the weather," Nancy said.

She gave the steering wheel a turn and headed the motorboat toward the eastern shore. Although it was not yet dusk, darkness seemed to be closing in upon the lake. It was with difficulty that the girls distinguished the shore line. The water, which only a few minutes before had been a smooth, clear blue, lashed about the little boat in angry, inky waves.

Helen studied the sky nervously.

"We'd better make full speed ahead, Nancy," she advised. "We're a long way from camp, and that big cloud is rolling up fast."

Nancy Drew was of the same opinion. One hasty glance at the cloud in question had assured her that there was no time to be lost if they were to beat the storm. Even before Helen had made the suggestion, she had opened the throttle to the fullest extent. The motorboat fairly leaped through the water, dashing spray into the faces of the two girls.

"Why didn't we start back a few minutes earlier?" Helen groaned. "We'll be drenched to the skin before we reach shore!"

"I'm afraid we shall," Nancy admitted. "I wonder if there are any oilskins aboard?"

"They may be under the seat. I'll look and see if I can find them."

A moment later Helen triumphantly brought out a mass of sticky yellow garments. She quickly slipped into a coat, and then relieved her chum at the wheel, giving her an opportunity to don the oilskins.

Hastily, Nancy pulled a southwester down over her curly, golden bob, and struggled into a coat several sizes too large for her. She was not an instant too soon, for suddenly a streak of forked lightning cut across the sky, momentarily disclosing a thick mass of ugly clouds. The lightning was followed by an ominous crack of thunder, which caused the girls to cower involuntarily.

"That was close," Helen murmured uncomfortably.

"It's just a taste of what's coming!" Nancy cried. "The storm is almost on us!"

The wind, which had been steadily freshening, now began to blow in earnest. It struck the boat with a force which caused Nancy to grasp the railing for support. Huge waves swept down upon the little craft, threatening to bury it.

Another dazzling flash of lightning illuminated the sky, and simultaneously a deluge of rain descended upon the unfortunate girls.

"Oh, this is terrible!" Helen wailed. "I can't see to steer!"

Nancy sprang to a position directly behind her chum and peered ahead into the darkness. As though by magic, the shore line had vanished. The blinding rain made it impossible to see more than a few feet beyond the bow.

"Hold to your present course!" she advised, shouting to make herself heard above the noise of the storm. "It can't rain like this for long."

The gallant little motorboat plowed defiantly through the waves, but the steady chug of its engine did not comfort the two girls. They knew that they were miles from camp, and should anything go wrong with the motor they would be entirely at the mercy of the waves. Nancy recalled that she had noticed only one fishing boat on the lake during the afternoon, and the knowledge that in case of an accident cries for help would go unheard did not add to her peace of mind. However, so long as the engine continued to labor faithfully, there was no need to worry.

"How much gasoline have we left?" Helen inquired anxiously.

"Oh, at least half a tank, Helen. We shan't need to worry on that score."

After a time the rain ceased to fall in torrents and a drizzle set in. However, the storm was by no means over, for the wind continued to blow a full gale and every instant it seemed to Nancy Drew and Helen Corning that the waves became higher.

"If only we could see where we're going!" Helen complained.

She had endeavored to maintain a straight course for the camp, but there was no way of estimating the amount of drift, and she had no idea how far they were from shore.

A jagged ribbon of lightning illuminated the path ahead. Catching her breath, Nancy Drew leaned forward and peered into the inky water. What she saw froze her with horror. Directly ahead, floated a big log!

"About!" Nancy cried frantically.

Helen, too, had seen the log which lay in the path of the motorboat, and the sight held her in a paralysis of fright. She "froze" to the wheel.

"About!" Nancy shouted again.

Helen gave the wheel a vicious turn. The boat responded, but not quickly enough. The log loomed up in the water ahead. With a splintering crash, the boat struck it.

The sudden impact of the blow threw Nancy Drew backwards. She went sprawling into the bottom of the boat. Helen, who still clung to the steering wheel, screamed in fright.

"Nancy, are you hurt?" she demanded fearfully.

Nancy did not reply, but hastily scrambled to her feet. With difficulty she managed to stand, for the boat listed sharply to the right. Instantly, she saw that the collision with the log had torn a jagged hole in the side of the craft. Water was pouring in through it.

"Quick!" Nancy ordered sharply. "We must bail or we'll sink!"

She sprang forward, and, tearing off her coat, tried to stuff it into the hole. Helen caught up a rusty pail which had been kept on hand for fish bait, and began to bail. She worked madly, but in spite of her efforts, the water came in faster than she could dip it out.

"Oh, it's no use!" she groaned. "We're sinking!"

Nancy, too, realized that they could not hope to stop the leak. The boat was doomed, and they with it unless aid came to them quickly.

"Shout for help!" she ordered. "Someone may hear us."

Cupping their hands to their lips, the girls shouted again and again.

"Help! Help!" they screamed desperately.

There was no answer. The wind howled derisively in their ears, mocking them in their plight.

"Oh, what shall we do?" Helen demanded hopelessly.

Already the two girls were standing in water over their ankles, and each instant the boat was settling lower. A big wave bore down upon them, and Nancy, who saw it coming, realized that it meant the end.

A deluge of water poured in over the sides.

"We're lost!" Helen cried. "We're lo——"

The words ended in a choking gurgle as the waters closed over her head.

CHAPTER II

A Desperate Struggle

As the motorboat settled into the lake, Nancy Drew leaped clear and began to tread water. Her first thought was for her chum. What had become of her?

Nancy Drew was an excellent swimmer. But, as Nancy knew, Helen Corning was barely able to keep herself afloat in a quiet pool. With crushing, smothering waves bearing down upon her, she would be helpless.

Frantically, Nancy glanced about. She heard no cry, but several yards away she thought she saw a white hand above the water. With powerful crawl strokes, she plowed through the waves toward the spot. The hand had vanished.

Bending at the waist and then suddenly straightening her body, Nancy shot down in a surface-dive. With eyes open, she groped about under water. At last she was forced to the surface, gasping for breath.

"Oh, I must find her!" she thought desperately. "I can't let her drown!"

Then only a few feet ahead, she saw her chum struggling. In her fright, Helen had forgotten what little she knew about swimming, and was thrashing madly about.

One powerful stroke brought Nancy directly behind her chum. Reaching out an arm, she hooked Helen under the chin, and with her free hand, elevated her body to the surface of the water. A huge wave bore down upon the girls, and before Nancy could secure a safe hold, Helen strangled and began to struggle. She clutched Nancy about the neck.

"Let go!" Nancy cried. "Let go!"

Helen, too frightened to realize what she was doing, only clung the tighter, carrying the two girls beneath the surface of the water.

At first panic took possession of Nancy Drew as she realized that Helen held her in a strangle hold. Then her mind cleared and she thought logically again. She had studied life-saving methods, and had been told how to break strangle holds. If only it would work now!

In a desperate attempt to free herself, she pushed with her hands against the side of her chum's face, at the same time attempting to raise one of the arms which imprisoned her. As she felt Helen's grip relax, she quickly ducked under the raised arm and came to the surface of the water directly behind her chum. Before Helen could clutch her again, Nancy snapped her into position for a safe carry.

"Don't struggle or we'll both drown," she warned Helen.

Feeling that she was safe, Helen relaxed somewhat. But scarcely had Nancy Drew begun to believe that she had her chum under control when a huge wave swept over the two girls. Again Helen began to struggle and fight. Although Nancy held her in a position from which she could not free herself, the battle was a wearing one.

"Hold your breath when you see a wave coming," Nancy instructed. "Don't be afraid. I won't let loose of you."

She knew that Helen would soon wear her out unless she overcame her fear and remained quiet. Already Nancy was short of breath, and for a swimmer far from shore that was a fatal warning. Yet never for a moment did she consider abandoning Helen, although by doing so she might save her own life.

Nancy Drew had no illusions concerning her situation. Excellent swimmer though she was, she knew it would be impossible to tow Helen ashore. Alone she might make it, but with her chum to consider, it was hopeless. If only she could manage to keep Helen afloat until help reached them!

The motorboat had sunk beneath the waves, and the log which might have given them temporary support had floated away in the dark-ness.

"Oh, if only that log would come in sight again!" thought Nancy.

As if in answer to her wish the log bobbed up at that instant, but before Nancy could grab hold of it it went out of sight. She watched eagerly, but it failed to reappear.

The exhausted girl's heart sank within her.

"Help!" Nancy cried frantically.

With a sinking heart, she realized that her voice would not carry far. She and her chum were at the mercy of the cruel waves.

In this moment when it seemed that there was no hope of rescue, it was but natural that Nancy Drew's thoughts should turn to her father. Would she ever see him again?

For the most part, Nancy's life had been an unusually happy one. Since the death of her mother many years before, she had lived with her father, Carson Drew, a noted lawyer en-gaged largely on mystery cases, in the Middle Western city of River Heights which was forty miles from Moon Lake. Aided by an elderly servant, Hannah Gruen, Nancy had taken over the direction of the household.

Her life had been an exciting one, for she had always taken an interest in her father's mystery cases. Carson Drew was proud of his daughter and openly boasted that she had a talent for unearthing mysteries and solving baffling cases.

Certainly Nancy Drew never missed an opportunity for a thrilling adventure. She had established herself as a clever detective by solving the mystery of a queer old clock. Her adventures in this connection are related in the first volume of the series, entitled, "The Secret of the Old Clock."

Later she had been involved in a rather weird mystery, one which carried her to a haunted house, there to aid two sisters, Rosemary and Floretta Turnbull. Nancy had discovered a hidden staircase, and it was through her efforts that the "ghost" of the Turnbull Mansion was captured. Her exciting adventures are recounted in the volume, "The Hidden Staircase."

Nancy had refused to accept a reward for her service, but in each case her friends had forced a token of remembrance upon her. Her trophies consisted of a mantel clock and a valuable silver urn. Her father had often declared that before she finished her career she would have the house cluttered.

Now, as Nancy Drew struggled to support her chum in the rough waters of Moon Lake, she wondered if her career was to come to a sudden end. How long could she manage to keep afloat? Certainly not for many more minutes.

Her heavy clothing dragged her down, her shoes seemed as heavy as chunks of lead. If only she could let loose of Helen for a minute, she could remove them.

"Can you float on your back for just a few minutes?" she asked.

"Oh, don't let go of me, Nancy," Helen pleaded. "I'm frightened to death!"

"I won't," Nancy promised.

She intended to remain with her chum until the end. After all, it did not greatly matter about the shoes, she told herself. Even were she rid of them, it would only prolong her time a few minutes. She could not hope to support Helen indefinitely. Each second dragged like an eternity.

At frequent intervals Nancy shouted for help, although she believed she was only wasting energy. Her breathing became increasingly difficult.

Helen Corning, who had gradually grown more calm, could not help but know that Nancy's strength was beginning to fail. For the first time she realized the sacrifice her chum was making. Encumbered as she was, she could never hope to reach shore.

"Save yourself," she begged. "Go on without me."

"Never!"

"You can reach shore alone, Nancy. If you try to save me, we'll both drown."

Nancy Drew knew that Helen spoke the truth, but she did not relax her hold. Nothing could force her to desert her chum. Each minute it seemed to her that she could not take another stroke, and yet, by sheer force of will, she managed to endure.

A huge wave bore down upon the two girls, smothering them in its embrace. Feebly, Nancy struggled back to the surface with her burden.

"One more like that and I'll be through," she told herself.

Just then she thought she heard a noise above the roar of the wind. Was it her imagination or had she really heard the splash of an oar?

"Help!" she screamed.

Was there really an answering cry or were her ears playing cruel tricks upon her? Again Nancy raised her voice in a frantic cry. This time there could be no mistake, for she distinguished the words.

"Hold on! I'm coming!"

Aid was coming at last! The thought gave Nancy Drew the courage to endure for a few minutes longer.

"Where are you?" a shrill voice called.

"Here! Here!" Nancy cried desperately.

Through the blinding rain she caught a glimpse of a dark object. It was a rowboat. If only she could hold out until it reached her!

As the rowboat approached, Nancy Drew fully expected to see it swamped. It swept toward the two girls on the crest of a wave, and only by dexterous use of the oars did the rescuer avoid crashing into them. There was only one occupant in the boat—a girl, and her puny strength availed but little against the wind and waves.

Twice she tried to bring the boat alongside the struggling girls, and failed. The third time, as the craft swept past, Nancy lunged and caught the side. She dragged Helen along, supporting her with one hand until she, too, secured a hold.

"Be careful or you'll upset the boat!" their rescuer shouted.

Nancy Drew was well aware of the danger, and she was at a loss to know how to climb aboard. Unless the boat were perfectly balanced, it would be certain to capsize at the first attempt the girls made to scramble over the side.

Swimming around the boat, Nancy Drew took a position directly opposite her chum.

"I'll try to balance it while you get in," she shouted.

As Helen attempted to scramble aboard

Nancy threw her weight to the opposite side. The craft wobbled uncertainly but did not upset. With the aid of the girl at the oars, Helen managed to reach safety.

It was more difficult to get Nancy into the boat, but at last she was dragged over the side. The deed accomplished, Helen collapsed on the bottom.

Nancy resisted the temptation to drop down beside her chum, for one quick glance at her rescuer assured her that the girl was nearly exhausted from her labors. Apparently, it was all she could do to keep the rowboat from being overturned. Tired as she was, Nancy Drew knew that she could not rest until shore was reached.

"Give me the oars!" she ordered. "You rest for a minute or two."

"I am about done up," the girl admitted. "When I heard your cries, I rowed out as fast as I could."

Nancy dropped down upon the seat and snatched up the oars.

"We couldn't have lasted much longer. You came just in time. But I won't try to thank you now. We're still in grave danger. Which way to shore?"

With a wave of her hand, the girl indicated the direction. She seemed too tired to speak.

Under Nancy Drew's powerful strokes, the

little boat plunged through the water. By skillful use of her oars, Nancy avoided some of the waves, but in spite of her efforts, the craft was battered about.

Each moment the wind increased in violence, hurling wild threats into the ears of the three girls. Could they outride the storm?

As the little boat was buffeted this way and that, it seemed to Nancy Drew that they were fighting a losing battle. The fear made her work more frantically than before.

CHAPTER III

A New Friend

Grimly, Nancy Drew applied herself to the oars, although she feared her efforts would be useless in the end. Her arms ached, and she was desperately tired. Chilled to the bone by the raw wind, hands numb with cold, she longed to give up the struggle. If only she could drop down in the bottom of the boat beside Helen and rest!

Yet, she could not give up, for she realized that the safety of her companions depended upon her work. She must keep on! As she doggedly bent to her task, the oars creaked protestingly in the locks.

It seemed to Nancy that an unkind fate had decreed the little boat was never to reach shore, for each instant the storm increased in violence. Gigantic waves lashed against the little craft, threatening to bury it. Each flash of lightning and clap of thunder struck the girls with terror.

The strange girl who had braved the elements to rescue Nancy Drew and Helen Corning, permitted herself only a brief rest.

18

Exhausted as she was, she snatched up an extra oar from the bottom of the boat and attempted to help with the rowing. Working in unison, the two girls sent the little craft leaping through the water. As they made progress against the wind and waves, Nancy took new hope.

"We'll make it!" she encouraged her companion.

A vivid flash of lightning illuminated the water, and directly ahead, through the rain, Nancy caught a glimpse of the shore line. A feeling of intense relief surged over her.

However, the battle was not yet won, for her companion shouted a sudden warning.

"The rocks! We must be careful or we'll be dashed against them!"

Scarcely were the words uttered when another flash of lightning disclosed the shore line more distinctly and, straight ahead, the ugly protruding nose of a jagged rock!

For an instant Nancy's heart leaped into her throat. Would they be dashed on that cruel rock over which the waves were dashing with high-sent spray?

"Oh, we'll be killed!" gasped the strange girl.

"To the left! To the left!" came the quick answer. "It's our only hope."

"We'll never make it," was the groaning reply.

"We must!"

It was a critical moment, and Nancy Drew's heart was in her mouth. But with a deft swerve of her oar she avoided the rock, and an oncoming wave swept them out of danger. Another five minutes and they were in the cove where the water was comparatively quiet.

"Safe!" Nancy murmured.

At last her oars struck a sandy bottom, and, promptly dropping them, she stepped out into water which reached nearly to her knees. Her fellow oarsman followed, and together they pulled the boat up on the beach.

Quickly, they helped Helen Corning to her feet. She was too weak to stand without a supporting arm.

"Oh, where are we?" Nancy cried desperately. "Isn't there some house near where we can take Helen?"

"There isn't a cottage within a mile," the strange girl informed her. "But there's a boathouse up the shore a little way. If we can get her there——"

"I can walk," Helen insisted weakly.

Supported on either side, she bravely demonstrated the truth of her assertion. Shivering with cold and excitement, the three bedraggled girls stumbled along the beach.

"Here we are!" the stranger called out presently.

Pausing before a well-built boathouse which stood a short distance from the water's edge, she flung open the door. In relief, Nancy and Helen entered.

"It's not a very comfortable place," the girl apologized; "but perhaps we can wait here until the storm is over. At least it's better than standing out in the rain."

Following Nancy and Helen inside, she closed the door.

"It's as dark as night," Helen complained.

"I'll try to find a lamp," the girl returned. "I'm sure there must be one here."

She groped about and after a little search found an oil lamp and a box of matches.

"That's better," she declared, as she placed the lighted lamp on the window sill. "We can see one another now."

Not without curiosity, Nancy Drew and Helen Corning surveyed their rescuer. She was a tall, slender girl, with delicately molded features and tragic brown eyes which still held a look of fright. Her dress, a severe black, was unrelieved by any trimming. Yet in spite of the simplicity of her drab garb, she was a pretty girl.

"We haven't thanked you for saving our

lives yet," Nancy began. "Why, we don't even know your name."

"My name?" the girl smiled. "I'm Laura Pendleton."

Nancy quickly introduced herself and her chum.

"It was fortunate for us that you came to our rescue when you did," she declared gratefully. "You heard our cries?"

"Yes. I had gone out for a walk along the shore when the storm came up suddenly. I was hurrying back to the hotel when I heard a shout for help. There was no one near by, and I didn't know what to do."

Laura nervously twisted her hands as she spoke.

"You found a boat?" Nancy prompted.

"Yes, fortunately there was one on the beach. But I was afraid to attempt the rescue alone."

"But you did," Nancy reminded her. "I don't wonder you were afraid to brave the storm."

"Oh, it wasn't just the storm. I'm afraid of water. I always have been. I can't even swim."

"You can't swim?" Nancy gasped. "And you risked your life to save us?"

"There wasn't any other way," Laura stated quietly. "I couldn't let you drown."

"Laura," Nancy said feelingly, "Helen and

I can't begin to tell you how grateful we are for what you did. You displayed real courage in rescuing us."

"It was splendid!" Helen added.

"Oh, I didn't do anything," Laura insisted. "I'm not very good at rowing a boat, and if luck hadn't been with me, I never would have reached you."

"Do you live near here?" Nancy questioned curiously.

A troubled expression passed over Laura Pendleton's face.

"I'm staying at the Lakeside Hotel. It's about a mile from here."

"You frequently take long walks?" Nancy encouraged her, for she sensed that something was worrying her new friend, and she hoped to draw out her story.

"I do when I'm lonely and discouraged," Laura answered soberly. She hesitated a moment and then added "You see, I've recently lost my mother."

"Oh," Nancy murmured gently. "I'm sorry. I didn't mean to remind you. I should have known——"

"I wanted to tell you. Sometimes it seems as though I must talk to someone. I'm so worried. There's no one to help or advise me."

"Your father?"

"He died nearly six years ago. I am an orphan."

"Surely you have friends to whom you can appeal?"

"I am afraid not. You see, mother was ill for a number of years before she died. We lived in hotels and I took care of her. Our social life was cut off."

"If there's any way that Helen and I can help, count on us," Nancy Drew announced firmly. "If you need money——"

"Oh, it isn't money," Laura said quickly. "Mother left an ample fortune. It's only that I'm lonely and discouraged and I don't know what my guardian will be like."

"Your guardian?" Helen questioned curiously.

"Yes. The court appointed Jacob Aborn. I've never seen him. He and mother were schoolmates."

"You dread to meet him?" Nancy asked gently.

"Yes. He's to come for me in a few days."

"Surely, if he and your mother were schoolmates, you have no cause for worry."

"I suppose I am silly," Laura admitted, "but I can't help it. I have the strangest feeling."

"What sort of feeling?" Nancy asked.

"Oh, I can't explain. It's just that I feel

that something dreadful will happen to me. I'm afraid to meet Jacob Aborn.''

"Perhaps he's the most kindly man in the world," Nancy declared. "When will he arrive?"

"That I don't know. I'm expecting him the latter part of this week. I received a letter from him last week telling me to wait at the Lakeside Hotel until he arrived. His letter was so curt and businesslike that it frightened me."

"I'm sure everything will come out all right," Helen assured her kindly.

"Oh, I'm probably worrying when there is no need," Laura said, forcing a smile. "You must pardon me for troubling you with my story."

"But we're interested," Nancy Drew protested. "I wish we could help you."

"Well, I don't need help yet," Laura laughed. "If I do, I'll probably call on you. By the way, I don't know where you live."

"Oh, we're spending a few days at a summer camp here on the lake," Helen informed her.

"Only a few days?"

"We'll be leaving next week," Nancy replied. "At least I will. However, I live at River Heights, which is only forty miles from here. I wish you could visit me there."

"I'd love to come, if my guardian will let me."

"And you must visit us at the camp," Helen added enthusiastically. "Why not come tomorrow afternoon?"

"Perhaps I can, if you really want me," Laura responded eagerly.

"Of course we want you," Nancy declared cordially. "However, I warn you that the girls will mob you when they learn you're a heroine."

Laura smiled timidly at her new friends.

"Perhaps you'll visit me sometime at my hotel?"

"We certainly will," Nancy assured her warmly.

Helen glanced toward the window and for the first time noticed that it had stopped raining.

"The storm is over," she announced.

"Then I must be getting back to the hotel before I catch my death of cold," Laura shivered. "I'm chilled to the marrow."

"So are we," Nancy commented. "This storm certainly brought cold weather with it."

"Won't you come with me to the hotel?"

"Oh, no, we must strike off for camp. The girls will be worried about us," Nancy Drew said hastily. "Thank you for your kind offer."

"But you'll take cold in those wet clothes."

"The sun is coming out, so we'll probably dry off before we reach camp. Anyway, you have a walk of nearly a mile before you, and it isn't much farther to camp."

"Then if you won't come, I'll say good-bye."

"Before we go we want to thank you again for saving our lives," Nancy told her earnestly. "I can't thank you adequately, but if ever I can be of service I hope you will call upon me."

"I certainly will," Laura assured her easily.

As the three girls gravely shook hands and parted, Nancy Drew little dreamed that before a fortnight had passed she would be given an opportunity to repay Laura Pendleton in full.

CHAPTER IV

A Visitor

"Do you think Laura Pendleton will visit us this afternoon, Nancy?"

Helen Corning, who was reclining on a camp cot in the little cabin which she shared with Nancy Drew, asked the question.

"I certainly hope so," Nancy responded. "I'd like to become better acquainted with that girl. She interests me."

"I wish we could repay her for saving our lives. I was so nearly done up yesterday afternoon that I didn't half thank her."

"I'm afraid there's nothing we can do, Helen. She has a fortune in her own name, so money would mean nothing to her. However, I thought she seemed rather lonely."

"Yes, she did," Helen agreed. "If she comes this afternoon we must show her a good time. Perhaps we can make her forget her troubles."

In spite of the severe exposure to which Helen and Nancy had been subjected the previous day, they were little the worse for their ducking in the lake. Upon reaching camp they

28

had removed their wet clothing and had gone to bed, with the result that they escaped without even a cold to remind them of their adventure.

Although the motorboat was not a valuable one, the girls regretted its loss and had generously offered to pay for it. However, the camp councilors had refused their money, exonerating them of all blame for the accident.

"I'm a little worried about Laura," Nancy Drew remarked to her chum. "She isn't at all strong looking, and I'm afraid she may be ill."

Helen did not reply, for just then a curly-haired girl thrust her head in at the cabin door and informed the two girls that they had a visitor.

"Oh, it must be Laura!" Nancy cried hopefully.

Helen sprang up from the cot, and, with her chum, rushed to the door. The girl who awaited them was indeed Laura Pendleton.

"I'm so glad you came," Nancy greeted her enthusiastically. "Helen and I were just talking of you."

"We were afraid you might be ill after that drenching," Helen added.

"I'm really stronger than I appear," and Laura smiled pleasantly. "I was fortunate enough not to take cold."

"We escaped, too," Nancy declared. "And now you must meet all of the girls."

Nancy Drew's friends crowded about and quickly were introduced to Laura. They made a great deal over her, and insisted upon regarding her as a heroine. The praise made little impression upon the girl, it seemed to Nancy. She noticed that while Laura was gracious to everyone, she took little interest in what was going on about her.

"Something is troubling her," Nancy thought.

At the urgent request of the campers, Laura joined in a lively game of volley ball which was in progress, but it was evident that she was not really enjoying herself. Nancy decided that it was time to take a hand.

"It's too warm to play volley ball," she informed her team mates. "Anyway, Helen and I haven't had a chance to talk with our guest."

To Laura's evident relief, the two girls bore her triumphantly away to their cabin.

"I'm afraid I'm dreadfully stupid at games," Laura apologized. "You see, I've never had an opportunity to enjoy sports."

"You're not stupid in the least," Nancy assured her warmly. "Who wants to waste a whole afternoon batting a silly ball over a net? I'm sure I'd much rather talk."

After politely presenting Laura with the only

chair which the tiny cabin boasted, Nancy and Helen "flopped" down upon the cots. At first the conversation was rather a two-sided one, for the visitor was somewhat shy, and it was evident that she was still unhappy over the death of her mother.

In an effort to direct Laura's thoughts into more pleasant channels, Helen began to tell her of some of Nancy Drew's thrilling adventures.

"She has quite a reputation as a detective," Helen declared impressively. "Everyone says Nancy can scent a mystery a mile away."

"What sort of mystery cases are you interested in?" Laura asked her new friend, in surprise.

"Oh, most anything," Nancy answered carelessly. "My father is a lawyer who is often engaged in such cases, and I suppose I get my liking for detective work from him."

"She makes a specialty of lost wills and haunted houses," Helen informed their guest mischievously.

"Haunted houses?" Laura gasped.

"Oh, the Turnbull mansion really wasn't haunted," Nancy hastened to explain. "The Turnbull sisters were bothered by strange noises at nights, and valuables kept disappearing from the house. I discovered who it was that was the ghost behind the scenes."

"Everyone said it was clever detective work," Helen went on proudly. "Nancy discovered a hidden staircase and an underground tunnel. She explored it in the dead of night."

"How exciting!" Laura declared. "Weren't you afraid?"

"A little," Nancy admitted truthfully.

"But she kept on, anyway," Helen continued. "Oh, she had a thrilling time of it before the mystery was solved!"

"I should think so," Laura murmured. "My, you must have talent, Nancy!"

"Not at all," Nancy laughed. "It was mostly luck that I stumbled upon that hidden staircase."

"Don't you believe it," Helen scoffed. "Nancy Drew's modest, that's all. She wouldn't tell you about the way she helped the Horner girls get their inheritance! They had been cheated out of a fortune, and Nancy unearthed the real will."

"Oh, Laura isn't interested in all that," Nancy protested, obviously ill at ease.

"Indeed I am," Laura assured her.

"We've been talking about ourselves so much that we haven't given you a chance to say a word."

"Oh, there's nothing to tell about myself. I'm not a very interesting person."

"Indeed, you are," Nancy Drew contradicted

her guest gently. "But I'm afraid you are still worrying about that guardian of yours. Am I correct?"

Laura's pretty face clouded.

"Yes, I am worried. I know I shouldn't feel the way I do, for it was my mother's wish that Jacob Aborn be appointed my guardian. I can't understand myself. I dread to meet him to-morrow."

"To-morrow?" Nancy questioned in surprise.

"Yes, I received a telegram from him this morning. He is to arrive to-morrow."

"I wouldn't worry," Nancy said cheerfully. "Probably you will like your guardian when you meet him. Surely, your mother wouldn't have entrusted you to his care if she hadn't believed he would be kind to you."

"Oh, it's just a silly notion on my part. I realize it, yet I can't rid myself of a feeling that something dreadful will happen to me."

Laura Pendleton arose and walked over to the window. She stood gazing out across the lake for a moment, and then resolutely turned and faced Nancy and Helen, who were regarding her anxiously.

"You mustn't mind my despondent moods," she told them, with a sad smile. "I promise you that if you will come to visit me at my hotel, I'll be more cheerful. Will you come?"

"We certainly will," Nancy and Helen declared together.

Laura hesitated a moment, and then added rather plaintively.

"I wonder—would you mind coming tomorrow?"

"Why, no," Nancy responded, in astonishment. "We'll be glad to come."

Laura's relief was evident. As she said good-bye she pressed Nancy Drew's hand gratefully. Then without a word of explanation, she left the two girls.

CHAPTER V

LAURA'S GUARDIAN

EARLY the following afternoon, Nancy Drew and Helen Corning, faithful to their promise, boarded a launch which made regular passenger trips, and were ferried to the Lakeside Hotel.

"I wonder if Laura's guardian has arrived yet?" Helen remarked curiously, as the two girls walked toward the hotel, which was one of the most exclusive on Moon Lake.

"We'll soon meet him if he's here," Nancy replied. "I do hope he's the right sort. Laura would be dreadfully unhappy with anyone who didn't understand her."

"She's frightened to death at the thought of meeting him. Do you imagine that was why she asked us to come here this particular afternoon?"

"Yes, I do, Helen. It was as plain as the nose on your face. To tell you the truth, I'm curious to meet Jacob Aborn."

The conversation ended abruptly as the two girls entered the hotel lobby. Nancy Drew made her way directly to the desk and after a brief wait was informed that Laura Pendleton would receive the girls in her suite. An elevator whisked them to the third floor.

Scarcely had they knocked on the door, when Laura opened it.

"Oh, I'm so glad you came," she cried. "I was afraid you wouldn't."

She led the girls into a pleasant suite. There was no need to ask if Jacob Aborn had arrived, for Laura's eyes disclosed that she was deeply troubled.

As Nancy stepped into the living room she saw the man slumped down in a chair near the window. When Laura politely presented him, he arose and grunted a "pleased to meetchu," without warmth. Nevertheless, his shrewd eyes swept the two girls appraisingly.

Jacob Aborn was a short, pudgy man, but apparently he lacked the good disposition commonly attributed to a fat man, for a tiny scowl lined his forehead. He was well dressed and wore a large diamond on his right hand.

"I was afraid I wouldn't get to see you girls again," Laura began hastily, when an awkward silence fell upon the group. "I'm leaving this afternoon."

"You're leaving Moon Lake so soon?" Nancy inquired, with a curious glance directed toward Jacob Aborn.

"Yes," Laura declared without enthusiasm.

"My guardian is taking me to Melrose Lake. That's a long way from here, isn't it?"

"Twenty miles I believe," Nancy responded. "I'm sorry you are leaving."

"So am I," Laura told her wistfully. "I like it here, and I was just beginning to get acquainted."

"Must you go so soon?"

"The air is much better at Melrose Lake," Jacob Aborn broke in. "Laura isn't in very good health, and it's my duty to take care of her. I promised her dear mother I would look after her."

"I never heard that Melrose Lake was particularly healthful," Nancy commented dryly.

"I have a fine bungalow there," Jacob Aborn added hastily. "That's another reason for leaving. It will be much nicer for Laura than living in a hotel."

"Possibly you are right," Nancy admitted reluctantly.

She had taken an instant dislike to Jacob Aborn, although she realized that she had no reason for her feeling. He seemed kind enough to Laura, and apparently deeply interested in her welfare. Yet at times his eyes had a hard, almost cruel, glint as he gazed upon her. Nancy was ashamed of her suspicion, yet she could not help but wonder if the man's affection for his ward was genuine.

Laura glanced nervously at her guardian. It was obvious that she was uneasy in his presence.

"Would you girls care to have tea in the garden?" she proposed hopefully.

"That would be lovely," Helen said quickly.

She, too, had taken a violent dislike to Jacob Aborn, and was eager for an opportunity to get away. It would be a relief to have a quiet talk with Laura.

However, Jacob Aborn had no intention of permitting Laura's plan to be carried into effect. He picked up his hat and bestowed a saccharine smile upon his ward.

"I will go with you, my dear."

It was clear to Nancy Drew that he was determined Laura should not have a chance to talk with her friends alone.

"Something is wrong," she thought. "Laura doesn't want to go to Melrose Lake, and he's forcing her to do it."

The afternoon was a failure so far as Laura Pendleton and her friends were concerned. They spent a miserable half hour over the tea cups, attempting to keep up a conversation. Laura's face was pale, and her eyes held an expression of fear.

Jacob Aborn appeared not to notice. He gulped his tea in one swallow, crumbled his cake upon the table cloth, and then, tilting back

his chair, proceeded to regale Nancy and Helen
with tales of his brilliant business ventures.
His stories, which were obvious untruths, disgusted the girls, but for Laura's sake they
listened politely.

"I'm going to make Laura's money earn
real interest," he boasted. "I'll invest it in
stocks. If you know the ropes you can beat
the market every time."

Nancy Drew raised her eyebrows in well-
bred disapproval.

"Will the court sanction such speculation?"

"The court? What's that got to do with it?"
Jacob Aborn demanded.

"As Laura's legal guardian, you will be responsible for the money and will have to make
an accounting," Nancy informed him. "My
father is a lawyer, so I know."

Jacob Aborn stared at her somewhat hos-
tilely.

"Oh, yes, to be sure," he muttered.

Pushing back his chair, he called loudly for
a waiter. Greatly to Laura's embarrassment,
persons at other tables turned and stared at
him curiously.

"Waiter! My check!" he ordered, with a
grand flourish.

The bill settled, he turned to Laura with sudden decision.

"You must get your things packed at once,

my dear. We are leaving in half an hour for Melrose Lake.''

''But you said we were to remain here until late this afternoon,'' Laura protested. ''I haven't had a chance to talk with Nancy and Helen.''

''I am sorry, but we must leave at once. Your friends will excuse you.''

''It doesn't seem right to rush away like this, when I invited you girls here to spend the afternoon,'' Laura apologized. She was on the verge of tears as she faced Nancy and Helen.

''We'll surely see you again some time soon,'' Nancy Drew promised.

''Oh, if you only will! You must come to Melrose Lake. I don't know a soul there and I'll be so lonesome.'' She turned to her guardian. ''What is the address? I want Nancy and Helen to have it.''

Jacob Aborn frowned.

''The address? Oh, they won't need it. Anyone can direct them to the bungalow.''

Nancy surveyed Laura's guardian curiously. Why was he so eager to get his ward away from them? From his response to Laura's question, she comprehended that he did not wish to encourage a visit to Melrose Lake.

''I'm afraid I must say good-bye,'' Laura told Helen and Nancy regretfully.

Soberly, the three girls shook hands. Laura clung to Nancy an instant, and as their eyes met it seemed as though she were trying to tell her something.

"We must hurry, my dear," Jacob Aborn put in impatiently.

With a show of affection, he carelessly permitted his hand to fall upon Laura's shoulder. Involuntarily, she cringed.

"Yes, I'm coming," she responded listlessly.

Without another word she turned and left the two girls. Jacob Aborn followed her into the hotel.

Thoughtfully, Nancy and Helen walked toward the dock to await the coming of the passenger launch.

"It's a shame!" Helen burst out after several minutes of silence.

"Yes, it is," Nancy Drew agreed. "I don't blame Laura for not wanting to go to Melrose Lake. She isn't going to be happy with *that* guardian."

"I think she's going to be miserable," responded Helen. "Why, that man is a perfect bear!"

At the dock the two girls learned that the ferry would not be in for fifteen minutes. So, rather than remain there, they strolled around the hotel grounds.

"That's the worst with choosing a guardian you haven't seen perhaps for years," was Nancy's comment as they walked along a path close to the side of the hotel. "Laura's mother when dying may have thought her old school friend was as he had been in their early years. On the contrary, he has changed for the worse."

The two girls walked along in silence for a minute. Then both came to a sudden pause.

"They're right over our head!" whispered Nancy excitedly. "Listen!"

The chums listened and were speedily made aware that they were directly under the second story windows of the two rooms occupied by Laura and her guardian. The guardian was in the girl's room and talking to her in anything but a pleasing manner.

"I said you would get your things packed at once," snarled Jacob Aborn. "And don't snivel any longer about those other girls and the way I treated them. I'm your guardian and after this you'll do as I say."

"I'll get ready," answered Laura meekly. "And please don't talk so loud or you'll upset the whole hotel."

"Never mind that," returned the man. "I'll be ready in ten minutes, and I want you to be ready too."

After that there was silence, and with a

meaning look between them Nancy and Helen turned and walked back to the dock.

"It's simply awful! I wish I could do something for her," said Nancy, shaking her head sadly.

CHAPTER VI

HOMEWARD BOUND

In the mad, happy whirl of camp life, Nancy Drew and Helen Corning were kept so busy that they had little time to think of Laura Pendleton and her troubles.

At first, Nancy had been inclined to worry about her, for she could not rid herself of the conviction that Jacob Aborn was not so kindly disposed to his ward as he pretended. But as the days passed and no word was received from Laura, she gradually faded into the background.

"There's nothing we can do to help her," Helen had summed up the situation. "The court appointed Laura's guardian, and unless he proves himself incompetent, there's nothing to be done about the matter."

"I'm afraid you're right," Nancy sighed.

The two girls became engulfed in an endless round of swimming, tennis, hikes, boating and handicraft work, and Laura was temporarily forgotten. Helen, after her unfortunate experience on Moon Lake, was determined to

44

learn how to swim, and Nancy undertook to teach her the crawl stroke. Each morning the girls spent several hours on the beach and in the water.

"I'm beginning to think that by the time I leave Moon Lake I'll be a real swimmer," said Helen with much satisfaction after a rather long lesson from Nancy.

"You certainly swim very well, Helen. But of course it takes practice to make perfect. I don't think you want to swim across the lake just yet."

"Across the lake! Well, I should say not! I think I'd be doing wonderfully well if I could swim from this dock to the one above here."

"You're going to do that to-morrow."

"Never!"

"Just wait and see."

On the morrow, much to her delight, Helen managed to swim not only from one dock to the other but to swim back again.

"I never thought I could do it," the girl declared in great delight. She was gasping a little for breath but her face was radiant. "Nancy, you're a great teacher. Any time you feel like giving up your idea of becoming a detective you had better become a swimming teacher."

"Thank you, Helen. That sounds nice. But

I think I'll stick to my hobby of solving mysteries."

So enjoyable was Nancy Drew's vacation at camp that she was induced to prolong her stay. But at last the day came when she announced that she must depart for home. In vain Helen coaxed her to remain.

"No, I must leave this afternoon," Nancy insisted firmly. "I've already stayed longer than I intended."

Directly after luncheon, to the keen disappointment of her friends, Nancy Drew backed her blue roadster from the shed which served as a make-shift garage. Tossing her suitcase into the back of the car, she regretfully prepared to depart.

"I don't see why you need to start so early," Helen protested. "Can't you stay a few hours longer?"

Nancy Drew shook her head.

"I have a forty-mile drive ahead of me."

"You can drive to River Heights in a couple of hours, at the most."

"If everything goes well. But I may be unlucky enough to get a flat tire. And look at those clouds!" Nancy indicated a mass of fleecy white clouds which had settled near the horizon.

"Oh, those aren't storm clouds," Helen declared. "It isn't going to rain."

"That's what we thought when we were out on Moon Lake in the motorboat," Nancy reminded her. "From now on, I'm taking no chances with storms. Especially when they come up as quickly as they do in this locality."

"Then why not wait another day, if you're afraid of the rain?" Helen teased.

"And get marooned here for a week! You know how the roads are after a storm."

"I can't blame you for not wanting to drive in mud," Helen admitted; "so I won't plead with you any more."

With a last good-bye, Nancy Drew started the engine. Girls stepped out of the way, and she skillfully backed the car to the main highway.

The road followed Moon Lake for a considerable distance, and Nancy drove slowly, enjoying a last glimpse of the shore. It was with regret that she left camp, for she had enjoyed every minute of her vacation. She loved the clear blue of the lake, the gigantic trees, the earthy odor of the forest, and the whisper of the wind in the pine needles.

Presently, emerging from the timber, the scenery was less interesting, and she made better time. Now and then, as she came upon a clearing, she cast an anxious glance toward the sky. Although the sun was shining brightly, Nancy Drew thought the clouds were becoming

blacker. Soon, she was convinced that a storm
was rolling up.

"Just my luck to run into one," she thought,
in disgust. "Well, I have chains with me,
anyway."

She glanced nervously at the speedometer
and was relieved to note that she was nearly
half-way to River Heights.

"There's no need to worry," she told herself. "I'll be home before the storm
strikes me."

Although Nancy Drew had never been afraid
of storms, her recent experience on Moon Lake
had made a strong impression upon her, and
now she stepped hard on the accelerator. The
little blue roadster went bumping over the ruts
at a rapid rate.

On down the road Nancy sped. Suddenly she
saw an obstruction in the path ahead, and hastily put on the foot brake. The roadster came
to a creaking halt before a huge sign which
read:

Detour.   Bridge out.   Take Melrose Lake
Road.

An arrow pointed to the left.

"How   aggravating!"   Nancy   exclaimed.
"Just when I'm in a hurry! Now I must travel

miles out of my way before I strike the River Heights road.''

Another anxious glance at the sky told her that there was no time to be lost. Already huge storm clouds had blotted out the sun.

"I'm going to be caught in the rain," she thought. "There's no escape."

Hastily, she backed the roadster and headed down the Melrose Lake detour. In spite of the need for haste, she dared not race the car over the rutty highway. She was forced to reduce her speed to less than twenty-five miles an hour, and even then it seemed as though the automobile would shake to pieces.

Presently, the winding road ahead became indistinct against the black background of the forest, for the storm clouds were nestling closer and closer to the earth. Nancy snapped on the headlights and two beams of light shot down the road, illuminating the rutty highway for a hundred yards ahead.

Instinctively, she grasped the steering wheel more tightly, and every nerve in her body seemed sensitized, for the uncertainty of her situation gave her a feeling of uneasiness. She wondered how she would ever reach the main road should the storm break and catch her in the forest.

The uncertainty was soon ended, for Nancy

saw great rain drops glisten down through the headlight beams. Then the drops became indistinguishable in a downpour of water that seemed to drop from an opened floodgate in the sky. The two deep ruts ahead quickly changed into swiftly rushing rivulets which spread out over the road in a wide sheet of water.

"This is terrible!" Nancy Drew cried. "If my wheels get down into those ruts, I'll be stuck!"

The roadster skidded from one side of the road to the other, several times barely missing the ditch. By a miracle, so she told herself, Nancy Drew avoided the deep ruts and kept the car moving.

Then, directly ahead, she saw a hill, and, low as it was, knew it could not be climbed without chains.

"There's no use trying to make it," she decided. "I must stop and put on chains."

Halting the roadster under a huge tree which offered a little protection from the pelting rain, she rummaged under the seat for an old slicker and a pair of galoshes. After putting them on, she pulled out the chains and grimly set to work.

It was not an enjoyable task, for the wheels of the roadster were covered with mud and the chains were stubborn. Nancy tugged and strained and wished with all her heart that someone would come along and volunteer to help her. However, the road was seldom traveled, and even the farmhouses were miles apart, so she was forced to depend upon her own resourcefulness.

"If it hadn't been for this hateful detour I'd have reached a paved road before the rain struck me," she grumbled.

Fastening the last chain, she gingerly removed her mud-coated galoshes, and with a sigh of relief climbed back into the roadster.

"Just in time, too," she told herself. "The worst of the storm is coming!"

Quickly starting the car again, Nancy Drew slowly crept up the hill and descended the slope in intermediate gear. Before she reached a level stretch, the storm broke in all its fury.

The trees along the roadside twisted and bent before the onslaughts of the rushing wind and a roar from the threshing branches welled up from the forest all about. The thunder crashed and went tumbling and rumbling down the uttermost parts of the sky, and lightning streaked up in brilliant zig-zags to the very dome of heaven.

"This storm is as bad as that one on Moon Lake," Nancy thought, in alarm.

In vain she watched the roadside for a farmhouse where she could seek shelter until after the rain. There was nothing to do but keep on.

The windshield became clouded, and it was with difficulty that Nancy made out the road ahead. It required close watching and quick thinking to keep the automobile wheels out of deep ruts. One mistake of judgment and the car would be mired down to the running board.

However, Nancy Drew was an excellent driver and had confidence in her ability to handle the wheel. The condition of the road caused her less worry than the vivid flashes of lightning. Sharp cracks of thunder on all sides, warned her that the lightning was close to the earth.

Suddenly a blinding tongue of savage lightning shot down directly in front of the roadster. There was a flash of fire and simultaneously a deafening roar. For an instant Nancy Drew thought the car had been struck.

Then came a splintering, ripping noise, and before the girl's horrified eyes a pine tree fell earthward. One glance told Nancy that the roadster was in its line of fall.

Frantically she slammed on the brakes.

CHAPTER VII

A Close Call

With a loud crash, the stricken pine tree fell across the road, directly in front of the blue roadster. The trunk struck the earth less than half a dozen yards from where Nancy Drew had brought the automobile to a sudden halt, and the branches touched the hood of the roadster.

For an instant, Nancy gripped the steering wheel, too stunned to comprehend fully how fortunate had been her escape from death. Everything had happened so quickly that there had been no time to become frightened until the danger was over. Now, as she considered what might have been her fate, she felt weak.

"If I hadn't slammed on those brakes when I did, it would have been too bad," she thought.

Ruefully, she surveyed the tree which blocked the road. What was she to do? In some way she must reach River Heights. If only someone would come along to help her!

"There probably isn't anyone within miles,"

she told herself. "If I get through, I must depend upon my own initiative."

The tree completely blocked the road, and as there was a steep ditch on either side, Nancy Drew saw at a glance that it would be impossible to pull out upon the bank. Fate had played an unkind trick upon her.

Gloomily, she put on her wet slicker and buckled on the muddy galoshes. As she stepped from the closed car a sheet of rain struck her in the face. Gingerly picking her way through the slush, she walked to the fallen pine and surveyed it critically.

The tree was a small one and Nancy thought that two men could move it quite easily. Unfortunately, the two men were not in evidence.

"If I could pull the trunk a little to one side, I ought to be able to get through," Nancy reasoned hopefully.

Grasping the branches, she tugged with all her might, but the tree did not budge. Next she attempted to lift the trunk, but only succeeded in tiring herself.

"Maybe I could roll it out of the way," she thought.

She pushed with all her might against the trunk, but the branches prevented it from rolling. This gave Nancy a new idea, and she fell to work pulling the branches out of the way.

At last she was forced to stop for rest. Unmindful of the rain which had now settled to a slow drizzle, she sat down on the trunk.

"It looks as though I'll be here all night," she mourned.

It was by far anything but comfortable on the wet trunk of the tree, and presently Nancy got up, shook herself, and climbed into the roadster. She was afraid that she would have to stay in that dismal place all night.

After a short while the rain let up a little, and feeling restless she again sought the tree trunk. Just then she heard a strange sound coming from behind her.

"If only someone is coming to help me!" she murmured to herself.

She strained her eyes and soon made out the object, which proved to be a large and shaggy dog. The animal, dripping with water, looked at Nancy in mild wonder and came to a halt.

"Come here, doggy," the girl cried. "Where is your master? Come here."

Instead of accepting this invitation the dog gave himself a vigorous shake which sent a shower of water over the girl and the roadster and then turned and loped away among the trees.

"Even that dog doesn't want to help me," Nancy told herself and smiled grimly.

Suddenly she sat up straight and listened. She could hear footsteps. Someone was splash-

ing through the mud and water, coming down
the road toward her.

"I hope it's someone who can help me," she
thought hopefully, as she sprang up from the
tree trunk.

As the stranger came within range of the
automobile headlights, she saw that it was a
girl. Nancy's sympathy went out to her as she
noted her bedraggled appearance.

"I beg your pardon," the girl began as she
rushed up to where Nancy was standing, "but
I'm in desperate trouble. Could you help me
reach River Heights?"

Nancy, who recognized the voice, could
scarcely believe her ears.

"Laura Pendleton!" she exclaimed.

The girl started violently as her name was
spoken. For the first time she peered intently
at Nancy.

"Oh!" she gasped in astonishment. "I
couldn't see your face against those bright
headlights!"

Nancy saw plainly that Laura was agitated
about something, and it was evident that she
had been running, for she was breathing hard.
She wore no head covering and the thin coat
which she had flung over her shoulders af-
forded little protection from the rain. Laura
was indeed a sorry sight.

"What is the matter?" Nancy demanded quickly. "Why, you're crying."

Laura sank down on the tree trunk and sobbed.

"Oh, everything, Nancy! Everything!"

Nancy Drew slipped her arm gently about the girl.

"You shouldn't be out in the storm," she chided her. "What is your guardian thinking of to let you expose yourself this way?"

"My guardian! Oh, I don't want to hear his name! I hope I never see him again!"

"You're not running away, Laura?"

"Yes, I am. I couldn't stand it another minute."

"You were trying to get to River Heights?"

"Yes, I thought you might help me. I've no other person to whom I can turn."

"Why, you poor dear!" Nancy comforted her. "Of course I'll help you. I haven't forgotten my promise."

"Then you'll take me away!"

"Just as soon as I can get this tree out of our path. I'm on my way to River Heights now, and you shall go with me."

"What are you doing on the Melrose Lake road? This is the most desolate place. I didn't think anyone came here unless he was forced to."

"That's why I came," Nancy informed her grimly. "There was a detour on the regular road. Then the storm caught me, and finally this tree! When the lightning struck it, I thought sure I was doomed."

"You must have had a narrow escape," Laura observed.

"Too narrow for comfort," and Nancy laughed shortly. "That tree didn't miss me by many feet! As it is, some of the branches are still touching the front of the car."

"What are you going to do, Nancy? Shall you be able to get through?"

"That's what I don't know. Are there any houses near here?"

Laura shuddered.

"My guardian's bungalow is only a mile away."

"Well, we won't call on him for help."

"Oh, if he'd find me here, I don't know what he'd do to me."

Nervously, Laura wrung her hands, and Nancy was afraid that she might have another fit of weeping.

"Jacob Aborn won't find you," she assured the girl.

"Oh, Nancy, you don't know what your kindness means to me," Laura cried gratefully. "You've promised to help me when you haven't even heard my story. I must tell you——"

"Not a word until we reach River Heights,"
Nancy broke in. "We must both get into dry
clothing as quickly as we can. Here, climb into
the car where the rain won't strike you."

"I'm soaked to the skin already. It doesn't
make any difference now."

"I must think of some way to get out of
here," Nancy said thoughtfully, more to herself than to Laura. "Do you think you're
strong enough to help me lift that tree? I
think maybe we can do it together."

"Oh, I'm sure we can," Laura declared
eagerly.

"Then let's try."

After pulling the branches away from the
roadster, the two girls tugged at the trunk.
Although the tree was a small one, it was re-
markably heavy for its size. Laura and
Nancy puffed and panted, but were rewarded
for their labors. Little by little they succeeded
in moving the tree a short way. Though pausing frequently to rest their arms, they kept at
the work.

"I believe I can get through now," Nancy
decided at length. "Let's try it, anyway."

The girls clambered into the roadster, and
Nancy started the engine. Proceeding cautiously at the very edge of the road, she drove
the car forward. Several small branches struck
the body and sides of the roadster, but did no

damage other than to scrape off a little paint.

"Well, we got through!" Nancy declared in relief. "Now for River Heights!"

"These roads are terrible," Laura commented anxiously. "Do you think we'll make it?"

"We'll be home inside of half an hour," Nancy assured her confidently, "and the first thing you must do when we get there is to change your wet clothing and go to bed. Just try to relax now."

Laura attempted to obey, but it was obvious that she was suffering from a nervous shock. Nancy Drew longed to question her concerning her troubles, but she felt it would be unwise, for Laura was on the verge of becoming hysterical. What she needed was quiet and rest.

There would be ample time to hear the story after they reached River Heights, Nancy told herself.

CHAPTER VIII

LAURA'S STORY

IT WAS nearly six o'clock when Nancy Drew's mud-splattered roadster finally reached River Heights and turned in at the driveway of the Drew residence. With a sigh of relief the two girls climbed from the automobile and stretched their cramped muscles.

The ride from Melrose Lake had been a tedious one, and Nancy's arms ached from the strain of holding the car to the road. She had been forced to battle mud until she had reached pavement a short way from the city. Laura Pendleton, who had been drenched by the chilly rain, was chattering with cold, and Nancy was far from warm.

"I'll find dry clothing for you right away," Nancy promised, rushing her friend toward the house.

As the girls entered, Hannah Gruen, the housekeeper, came from the kitchen and surveyed them in amazement.

"Land sakes!" she exclaimed. "You must have been caught in the storm!"

"We certainly were," Nancy returned. "Hannah, this is my friend, Laura Pendleton. We're both soaked to the skin. While we're changing into dry clothing, I wonder if you would make us some hot tea or a little beef broth?"

"Indeed, I will," Hannah assured her eagerly.

"Is father here?" Nancy questioned, as the housekeeper started toward the kitchen.

"Mr. Drew left for St. Louis early last week."

"Oh, I didn't know he was going." Nancy was disappointed, for she had hoped that her father would be at home to meet Laura. "Business, I suppose?"

"Yes, I think he said it was about some law case. He left a note for you. I'll get it."

The housekeeper hurried to the desk. Removing an envelope from a drawer, she handed it to Nancy.

"You'd better change your clothes before you read it," she advised the girl.

Nancy took Laura upstairs and quickly found suitable garments. As Laura was about her own size, she had no trouble in fitting her. While she dressed, Nancy scanned the note from her father.

"He was called away unexpectedly," she told Laura. "I'm sorry he isn't here, because he will want to thank you for saving my life.''

''Oh, I don't want any thanks for that,'' Laura protested.

''Father says he will get back either to-morrow or the next day, so perhaps you'll meet him after all.''

''Oh, I can't stay that long, Nancy.''

''Nonsense! I won't permit you to leave until I'm certain you've suffered no bad effects from this adventure. Do you feel better now?''

''Yes, I'm all right.''

''Then we'll go downstairs. Hannah will have something for us to eat.''

''What a beautiful home you have here, Nancy!'' exclaimed Laura as she looked around her with much satisfaction.

''I think it's nice, Laura,'' answered the lawyer's daughter. ''Anyway, it's very comfortable. Dad and I wouldn't like it any better.''

''I had just such a nice home once,'' returned the visitor, and her voice saddened a bit. ''That was when mother and dad were alive.''

''Well, I hope that some day you'll have just as nice a place in which to live,'' and Nancy placed an assuring hand on the other girl's shoulder.

After a warm meal, Nancy lighted a small fire in the fireplace and insisted that Laura curl up in a comfortable chair and toast her feet.

"Just relax," she ordered.

Laura leaned her head back against the cushions and gave a tired sigh.

"Oh, it's so homelike here, Nancy." Her voice broke. "I'm afraid I'll never have a happy home again—now that mother is gone."

"Perhaps you'll feel better if you tell me what is troubling you, Laura."

"Oh, it's my guardian, Nancy. I can't live another day with Jacob Aborn."

"Isn't he kind to you?"

"Kind!" Laura's eyes flashed. "He doesn't know the meaning of the word! I don't see why mother ever placed me under his guardianship."

"Tell me what has happened since you left Moon Lake, and perhaps we can think of a way out of your difficulties."

"Jacob Aborn is so dictatorial and mean," Laura began. "He was fairly decent to me as long as we were at Moon Lake, but just as soon as we reached his bungalow he came out in his true colors."

"I wasn't favorably impressed with him myself," Nancy Drew admitted. "Didn't he take you to a nice home?"

"Oh, the bungalow is all right. I haven't any complaint on that score, save that it's very far removed from the other cottages on the lake. But, Nancy, would you believe it? He doesn't keep a single servant."

"He didn't expect you to do the work?"

"He did, Nancy. And the bungalow has nine rooms, too. I hadn't been there an hour when he told me to get busy."

"How mean! Why, you're not strong enough to do hard work," Nancy protested. "I thought your mother left an ample allowance for your needs."

"I thought the same, but it seems I was mistaken."

"Jacob Aborn told you that?"

"Yes. I had understood that mother left something like fifty or sixty thousand dollars. My guardian tells me the estate has dwindled to less than fifteen thousand dollars."

"Even that amount should be sufficient to keep you, Laura."

"Jacob Aborn says it wasn't wisely invested. He claims I'm not much better off than a pauper."

"Strange he should wait until he had taken you to Melrose Lake before he told you," Nancy murmured in so low a tone that Laura did not hear.

"Oh, you have no idea how I've suffered the last few days, Nancy. Jacob Aborn has been so hateful to me. He won't give me any spend-

ing money, and he says I'm not to have any
more money for clothes."

"I don't wonder you couldn't stand it."

"You haven't heard the worst. He even
took my fur coat away from me. I hadn't had
an opportunity to put it in storage and had it
in my trunk."

"He took your coat?" Nancy gasped.

"Yes. I think he intends to pawn it."

"I never heard of anything more out-
rageous!"

"And he's been trying to force me to turn
over mother's jewels to him."

"You didn't do it!" Nancy exclaimed
quickly.

"No, they're wrapped up in that little bundle
I brought with me. Perhaps I can put them
in your safe for a few days?"

"Certainly."

"The jewels are worth considerable, though
of course I wouldn't think of selling them."

"What did Jacob Aborn want with them?"
Nancy questioned suspiciously.

"He said he intended to put them in a safe
place, but I didn't believe him. I feel sure he
expected to sell them."

"That man must be a regular villain,"
Nancy observed indignantly.

"He threatened me, too. He said if I didn't
turn over the jewels he'd lock me up in my

room. I can't understand the man, Nancy. He does the queerest things."

"What sort of things, Laura?"

"Well, for one thing he leaves the bungalow every night, carrying a small bundle. When he returns, the bundle is gone."

"That is odd," Nancy said thoughtfully. "How long is he usually gone?"

"Oh, about an hour I should judge. I haven't the slightest idea where he goes, but he acts as though he's afraid someone will see him," she answered.

"It does look peculiar, Laura. Have you noticed anything else about him?"

"He always makes these trips after dark when he thinks I'm asleep. Several times I've heard him steal out of the house."

"You never followed him?"

"Mercy, no! I'd have been afraid. Anyway, I couldn't have done it had I wished, because he always locked me in."

"H-m," Nancy mused thoughtfully. "He must be afraid you'll learn something."

"Either that or he wanted to prevent me from running away."

"How did you manage it?"

"Jacob Aborn seldom leaves the bungalow in the day time, but this afternoon was an exception. He locked me in my room and left me there. Just as soon as he was out of sight,

I bundled up mother's jewels—I had hidden them under the mattress. Then I made a rope out of the sheets and lowered myself to the ground. I started off down the road, hoping I would meet someone who would help me reach River Heights."

"How fortunate that I ran into you."

"Yes, it was. The storm came up quickly and I was dreadfully frightened. I knew Jacob Aborn would half kill me if he caught me. Now that I have escaped, I don't know what I had better do. Can I be forced to return to that horrible man?"

"Are you sure he's your legal guardian?"

"I guess he is," Laura admitted miserably. "I saw the papers."

"Unless the court appoints a new guardian I am afraid he could force you to return," Nancy said slowly. "Of course, I'm not sure about that, but I believe he would have a legal right to do it. I wish father were here. He would know."

"Oh, what shall I do, Nancy?" Laura cried desperately. "I can't go back! I'd sooner be dead!"

"Don't worry," Nancy said comfortingly. "Jacob Aborn hasn't found you yet."

"But I have no place to hide. I am without friends."

"You mustn't forget that I am your friend,"

Nancy returned quietly. "I'll do everything in my power to help you."

"Oh, Nancy, you're so good." Tears came into Laura's eyes.

"You mustn't think about Jacob Aborn any more. You are to stay here until my father comes back. He'll be able to help you, I know. Perhaps I'll be able to think of something myself."

A look of determination settled over Nancy Drew's face. She was convinced that Jacob Aborn was a cruel guardian, and she intended to help her new friend. If only she could think of a way!

CHAPTER IX

NANCY'S PLAN

AT BREAKFAST the following morning, Nancy Drew was gratified to observe that Laura Pendleton appeared happier and less nervous than on the night before. A little color had crept into her thin cheeks, and in the bright gown which Nancy had loaned her, she looked like a different girl.

"Did you sleep well?" Nancy inquired, as the two sat down at the breakfast table.

"Much better than I have for the past week. I guess I can't help worrying about things."

"You have a great deal to trouble you, Laura," Nancy said quietly, after Hannah had deposited a plate of waffles before the girls and had returned to the kitchen. "I've been thinking about what you told me last night, trying to find a way to help you."

"I was overwrought, Nancy. I shouldn't have inflicted my trouble upon you."

"Laura, don't you understand that you're not inflicting anything upon me?" Nancy questioned gently. "I owe you a debt greater than

I can pay. You're welcome to remain here as long as you will. And I believe I know of a way to help you. You haven't changed your mind about going back to live with your guardian?"

"Oh, no! I will not go back unless I'm forced to it."

"Good! Then I'll tell you of my plan. I am anxious to talk with your guardian again. You write a letter to him and I'll deliver it. That will give me my chance."

"Aren't you afraid to go near him?"

Nancy shook her head.

"He may harm you."

"He wouldn't dare."

"Oh, you don't know that man, Nancy! If he thinks you helped me escape, he may do anything!"

"He'll not learn anything from me, Laura, and by talking with him I may learn something important. Will you write the note?"

"Yes, if you're determined to go through with it."

"It's the only way I know of meeting him again, Laura!"

"But the risk!"

"I don't believe I'll be in any real danger."

"Jacob Aborn's cottage is located in such an isolated spot, Nancy. If anything should happen to you, there would be no one to help you.''

''I'll be cautious.''

''There's another reason I hate to have you go,'' Laura added, with a troubled frown. ''I'm afraid my guardian will find out where I am staying. Then he'll come after me.''

''I'll take care that Mr. Aborn doesn't learn you're staying with me.''

''When do you want me to write the letter, Nancy?''

''Any time this morning. I'll wait until afternoon before I start for Melrose Lake. That will give the roads a chance to dry.''

The two girls finished their breakfast and then went to the study, where Nancy helped Laura compose the letter to Jacob Aborn.

''What shall I say?'' Laura questioned.

''Tell him that you refuse to accept him as your guardian,'' Nancy dictated, ''and that you will not return until you have a court order. Oh, yes, it might be well to add that you've placed the matter in the hands of a lawyer. That's really the truth, because I know father will take your case just as soon as he gets back from St. Louis.''

''Jacob Aborn will just go wild when he gets this letter!''

''Let him. I'm curious to see how he will react.''

"How about the jewels I brought with me? Shall I put them in the safe now?"

"Yes, we'll do it right away. They're probably safe enough in the house, but we'll take no chances."

Laura hurried upstairs and soon returned with a small parcel which she handed to Nancy. The latter opened the wall safe, and after placing the package inside the tiny vault closed the door and turned the dial.

"Father and I are the only persons who have the combination," she explained to Laura, "so I know your jewels will be perfectly safe."

Directly after luncheon, Nancy Drew prepared to depart on her mission. Somewhat reluctantly, Laura said good-bye, and it was evident that she was afraid to have her friend visit Jacob Aborn.

"Do be careful," she warned.

"I will," Nancy promised.

"When shall I look for you back?"

"Oh, late this afternoon or early to-night. I'll make the trip as quickly as I can, but I imagine the roads will be rough and that will slow me down some. If anything should happen that I can't get back to-night, I'll telephone."

"I'll worry every minute you're away."

"You mustn't do that," Nancy chided her. "Try to enjoy yourself. You'll find a number of interesting books in the library, and if you want anything just ask Hannah.''

"I will,'' Laura returned soberly.

"Then I'm off!''

With a friendly wave of her hand, Nancy Drew guided the roadster down the driveway. After weaving her way through city traffic, she reached the outskirts and took the road to Melrose Lake.

"Poor Laura!'' she thought as she drove along. "She's so nervous and worn out. I don't wonder, when she has so much to bother her. I hope I can help.''

As Nancy Drew considered Jacob Aborn's strange attitude toward his ward, a troubled look came into her eyes. She could not understand the man's unkindness to Laura, for certainly she was a lovable girl. And was it really true that the Pendleton estate had dwindled to a paltry fifteen thousand dollars?

"I intend to find out for myself, if I can,'' she told herself resolutely. "It strikes me there's something rather peculiar going on at Jacob Aborn's bungalow.''

Aside from her desire to help Laura, the girl's problem had caught Nancy's interest. She had taken a dislike to Jacob Aborn the first time she had met him, and had sensed his eagerness to get Laura to his bungalow at Melrose Lake. Even before she had learned what had happened there, she had been suspicious of the man. His bad manners and occasional slips of grammar puzzled her a bit.

"There's something strange about those midnight excursions of his, too," Nancy thought. "I wonder what he carries in the bundle Laura was telling me about."

In spite of her eagerness to reach the bungalow, Nancy Drew was forced to travel slowly, for although the road was practically dry, it was extremely rough. She jounced about uncomfortably in the seat.

After a time she came to the Melrose Lake detour. As she turned down into the narrow, winding road, she found it necessary to go even more slowly. Few automobiles had passed over the road, and it was in worse condition than the one she had just left. In places where a canopy of trees prevented the rays of the sun from striking, the ground was still wet.

"At least I won't need to worry about getting the car splashed," Nancy chuckled.

The blue roadster was blue in name only, for the mud of the day before still clung to it. There had been no time between trips to have it washed.

Presently Nancy approached the spot where the pine tree had fallen, and to her satisfaction she saw that it had been pulled to one side so that the road was no longer obstructed.

Now, as she drew near the turn-off which she must take in order to reach the Aborn bungalow, she drove more slowly, lest she inadvertently miss it. Sighting the road, she turned into it.

She had gone but a few rods when she chanced to look toward the right. Through the trees, she caught a glimpse of a man walking rapidly away from the road. He carried a small bundle under his arm.

"Jacob Aborn!" Nancy exclaimed.

Impulsively, she switched off the motor of her roadster and sprang to the ground.

CHAPTER X

ABANDONING her automobile, Nancy Drew
hurried across the road and without an instant's hesitation plunged into the thicket
where she had just caught a fleeting glimpse
of a man she believed to be Jacob Aborn. She
had acted upon the impulse of the moment, and
had not stopped to consider what might be the
outcome of her daring.

Fortunately, the man had failed to note the
approach of Nancy's roadster, and was unaware that he was being followed. Without
turning his head or looking back, he trudged
down a path which led deeper into the forest.

Although Nancy was unable to see the man's
face, she recalled the peculiar stoop of his
shoulders and his manner of walking. There
was no doubt in her mind as to his identity.
Even had he not been carrying a small bundle,
she would have been certain that it was Laura's
guardian.

"I wonder where he's going with that package?" she questioned herself. "Here's where

I play sleuth and see what I can find out."

Following at a safe distance, she managed to keep the man in sight. He walked swiftly through the timber. Once, however, as a stick crackled under Nancy's feet, he turned and looked back. Only by quickly ducking behind a bush, did Nancy save herself from detection. Jacob Aborn listened intently for a moment, and then, muttering to himself, continued through the forest.

"I'd better be more careful if I don't want to get caught," Nancy warned herself.

After that she trailed Jacob Aborn more cautiously, keeping farther back. Where was the man going? Certainly not to his bungalow on the lake, for Laura had told her that was in the opposite direction.

Presently, Nancy saw him disappear behind a clump of bushes. When she reached the spot, the man had vanished. In vain she looked about in all directions. Jacob Aborn seemed to have disappeared into thin air.

"That's strange," she murmured. "I'm sure he came this way."

It occurred to her that possibly the man had become aware that he was being followed and had hidden in the bushes to watch. The thought made Nancy uneasy, for she realized that unwittingly she might walk into a trap. While she was not exactly afraid of Jacob Aborn, she had no desire to have him learn that she was spying upon him.

Alert for possible danger, she moved forward with the utmost caution. She paused frequently to listen, but there was no sound in the bushes. What had become of Jacob Aborn?

With great caution the girl moved from one bush to another. She looked at all the trees in the vicinity, but not one of them hid the form of the man.

"Gracious! it looks as if he'd been swallowed alive," thought the girl.

She examined the ground, almost expecting that there would be some cave or secret tunnel in that vicinity. But the ground was firm and in many places very rocky.

Not knowing what to think of the strange disappearance, she went forward slowly and cautiously, following the general direction the man had previously taken.

Then, unexpectedly, Nancy Drew plunged through the bushes and stepped out into a tiny clearing. To her amazement she saw before her a small bungalow which had fallen into a state of decay. The windows had all been boarded up, and the roof sagged. The yard was choked with weeds.

"One good gust of wind would blow the place over," Nancy told herself. "This can't be the Aborn bungalow where Laura lived with her guardian. I wonder who owns the place.''

She stood in the shadow of the trees, curiously surveying the structure. A suspicion began to creep into her mind. Was it possible that Jacob Aborn had entered the building? If not, what could have become of him? Nancy was certain that he was not in the forest, for there was no sound in the bushes.

''What would Jacob Aborn be doing here?'' she wondered. ''There's something peculiar about it.''

Just then Nancy chanced to glance down toward the ground. Directly ahead, in the soft earth, she saw the print of a man's shoe. Instantly, her suspicions were confirmed. She was firmly convinced that Jacob Aborn had come this way.

''I'll just have a look at that bungalow,'' she decided.

With a quick glance about to make certain that she was not being watched, Nancy hurried toward the cottage. As she approached, a large sign at the front of the building brought her up short.

The placard, which was printed in bold uneven letters, read:

Keep Off This Property.

Nancy studied the warning a trifle uncertainly, and then shrugged her shoulders.

"I'm not afraid! It will take more than a sign to scare me away!"

The bungalow appeared deserted, but Nancy suspected that Jacob Aborn was somewhere in the vicinity, for otherwise she could not account for his sudden disappearance. She must keep a sharp watch for danger, she told herself. It would not do to be caught spying. Laura had warned her that her guardian was a dangerous man when aroused.

Tiptoeing across the front porch, Nancy quietly tried the door. It was locked. Undaunted, she proceeded to the rear door and found that it was likewise securely fastened.

Although disappointed, she was unwilling to give up. Making a complete circuit of the bungalow, she saw a window from which several boards had fallen. Returning to the rear of the building, she found a small box and dragged it to a position directly beneath the window. By standing upon it, she would be able to peer into the bungalow.

With a last cautious glance in all directions, to assure herself that her actions had not been observed, Nancy Drew mounted the box. Pressing her face against the glass, she gazed inside. The room into which she looked was bare of furniture and covered with dust, but there was nothing unusual in its condition. Any house which had been deserted for several months would have appeared similar.

"I wish I could get inside," Nancy thought.

She was about to climb down from the box when a strange feeling came over her. Though she had heard no sound, she sensed that unfriendly eyes were watching her every move.

Before she could turn around and look over her shoulder, a coarse, angry voice barked into her ear:

"What are you doing here?"

In surprise and fright, Nancy Drew nearly fell from the box.

She wheeled and faced Jacob Aborn.

CHAPTER XI

ORDERED AWAY

"WHAT are you doing here?" Jacob Aborn repeated harshly. His eyes burned with rage, and for an instant Nancy Drew believed that he intended to strike her.

With as much dignity as she could command, she stepped down from the box and regarded him coldly.

"Why, just at the moment, as you probably observed, I happened to be looking in at the window," she said easily.

Although outwardly calm, Nancy was doing some rapid thinking. She realized that she had placed herself in an awkward position and must keep her wits about her. As she answered Jacob Aborn, her tone of voice infuriated him more than ever. He came a step nearer, his eyes blazing.

"What right have you to be looking into other people's houses?"

"I was merely curious," Nancy replied. "I didn't know the bungalow was inhabited."

"Who said it is?" Mr. Aborn demanded

hastily.   Nancy thought that an expression of alarm had come over his face.   "Get away from here quick! This is private property!"

"Your property?" Nancy inquired.

"It's none of your business whose property it is! You have no right here! Can't you read signs?"

"It seems to me I did see one at the front of the bungalow."

"Then if you know what's good for you, get away from here!"

As Nancy made no move to depart, Jacob Aborn became more abusive.

"Get away from this bungalow, I tell you! I want no sneak thieves around!"

"Now just a minute, Mr. Aborn!" Nancy's voice was quiet, but it held a quality which warned the man he had gone too far.   "I'll not permit you to call me a sneak thief. When you get through ranting around, I'll tell you why I came here."

"Humph!   It's probably a trumped-up story."

"I thought you might be interested to learn what became of your ward, Laura Pendleton, but since you don't wish—" She turned as though to move away, although she had no intention of doing so.

As she had expected, Jacob Aborn's curiosity was aroused.

"Hold on there!" he stopped her. "You say you have news of Laura?"

"If you're ready to listen, I'll tell you. I came to Melrose Lake this afternoon to see you. I was driving toward your bungalow when I saw you walking through the woods. I stopped my car and followed——"

"You followed me?" Jacob Aborn hissed. His face had suddenly become convulsed with anger.

"Oh, I lost track of you in the timber," Nancy said hastily. "I came to this bungalow, and I didn't know where you had gone."

Watching the man closely, she saw that his tension relaxed somewhat. Evidently, he had been afraid that she had learned too much.

"What about Laura?" he demanded.

"I was coming to that. I have a note which she asked me to deliver to you."

"Hand it over."

Nancy fumbled in her pocketbook and at last produced the letter which she and Laura had composed. Jacob Aborn snatched it from her hand and eagerly ripped open the envelope.

As he read the message, Nancy Drew watched him closely. Now that he was no longer attempting to mask his emotions, she observed that his face was hard and cruel. No wonder Laura hated him!

As Nancy studied the man, she noticed with

a start that his bundle was gone. What had become of it? He had been carrying it only a few minutes before. She wondered where he could have hidden it so quickly.

The message did not add to Jacob Aborn's good humor. As he scanned the letter, an expression of bitter hatred settled over his face and his eyes narrowed to mere slits.

"So Laura's turned her case over to a lawyer, has she?" he snarled. "A lot of good it will do her." He wheeled upon Nancy. "Tell me where she is."

"I can't tell you that."

"You know where she is all right."

"Perhaps I do, and perhaps I don't."

"You induced her to run away," the man snarled.

"I did not! Laura ran away of her own accord. She said you were unkind to her."

"Bah! Laura is ungrateful. I am doing all I can for her because of my friendship with her mother. This is the way she repays me."

Nancy made no response, and Jacob Aborn continued angrily:

"That's what I get for taking in a poverty-stricken orphan. You say she told you I didn't treat her kindly?"

"Yes, she did."

"She told you a lie. I've treated her like my own child. I've given her everything. Now

I'll tell you something about that ward of mine." A crafty light came into Jacob Aborn's eyes. "At times she's a wee bit unbalanced—thinks folks don't treat her right."

"Indeed?"

"Yes, Laura's mighty queer. It's for her own good that I must get her back. She needs the care of someone who loves her. Now you're her friend and want to help her. You can do it if you will."

"How?"

"By telling me where she is."

Nancy laughed shortly.

"I'll not tell you a thing! I can see through your little scheme! You want to get your hands on Laura's money."

"Money!" the man cried scornfully. "If it wasn't for me Laura wouldn't have a cent. The estate has dwindled to almost nothing. It's only out of the kindness of my heart that I took her in."

"How much did the estate amount to?" Nancy questioned shrewdly.

"I can't say off hand, but there's nothing left now. Laura is a pauper. And what's more, she's a thief."

"A thief!"

"Yes, that's what I said. When she left here, she took some valuable jewels with her. They belong to me, and I want them back!"

For an instant Nancy Drew was aghast. However, she had faith in Laura, and believed in her honesty. She was a keen judge of character, and a look into Jacob Aborn's face convinced her that he was lying.

"How dare you say anything like that about Laura?" she cried angrily.

"It's the truth. By refusing to tell where she is, you're harboring a criminal."

"Laura a criminal? It's ridiculous."

"Laura is my ward. I have a legal right to her. Will you tell me where she is?"

"I gave you my answer once. I will not!"

"Oh, you won't, eh? Well, I'll find her all right. And when I do, I'll turn the police on her. Now get away from here!"

As Nancy hesitated, uncertain what to do, Jacob Aborn picked up a stick from the ground and started toward her menacingly.

"Move!" he ordered harshly.

Nancy Drew backed away, for she saw that he intended to harm her if she continued to defy him. Turning, she ran swiftly toward the timber.

"Hi! Come back here!" exclaimed Jacob Aborn. "Come back! I want to talk to you!"

Nancy paused in her flight.

"What do you want now?"

"Perhaps we can come to terms."

"What kind of terms?"

"I might make it worth your while to tell me all about Laura," said the man ingratiatingly.

"Oh, indeed? If that's the sort of person you are, Mr. Aborn, you'll get nothing out of me," returned Nancy indignantly.

"Then you clear out, and clear out quick," roared the irate man and took several steps toward her, flourishing his stick menacingly.

"You dare touch me and you'll wish you hadn't!" returned Nancy defiantly.

Yet she thought that prudence would be the better part of valor and so she kept on toward the timber and was soon out of sight of the man who kept gazing after her in a manner that showed his evil disposition.

CHAPTER XII

NANCY BIDES HER TIME

NOT until she had reached the blue roadster which stood waiting at the edge of the forest did Nancy Drew pause in her flight. As she climbed into the automobile, she cast a glance over her shoulder and was relieved to see that Jacob Aborn had not followed her.

"I believe that man intended to strike me," she thought grimly. "He became positively vicious when I refused to tell him where Laura is. It's plain that he intends to get her back if he can, and it's up to me to prevent it. I'm not sure what his game is, but I intend to find it out!"

Nancy started the motor, and after backing around in the narrow road, drove slowly toward the main highway. She felt that she had made a number of important discoveries concerning Laura's queer guardian, but just how she could utilize the information she did not know.

She was inclined to believe that there was something rather mysterious about the de-

serted bungalow in the woods. What was Jacob
Aborn doing in the vicinity and why had he
been so afraid that she would investigate the
place?

"He's up to mischief, that's certain," she
told herself, "and it bodes no good for Laura
Pendleton."

Not for a minute did Nancy Drew believe the
charges Jacob Aborn had made against his
ward. She was convinced that he had made
them in order to induce her to tell him where
Laura had gone.

"I don't know what to do," she thought.
"I don't want to leave Melrose Lake until I
have learned something that will help Laura.
Unless I do, that man may find out she is staying with me and force her to return. I suppose
he would have a legal right to do that."

As Nancy drove slowly along the road, she
turned the perplexing problem over in her
mind. At last an idea came to her.

"Why didn't I think of it before? I'll go
to one of the hotels on the lake and engage a
room. Then after it gets dark I'll do a little
investigating."

Nancy recalled that Laura had told her there
were several nice hotels a few miles farther
on, and at once she determined to stop at the
first one she came to. Presently she approached the Beach Cliff Hotel, and as it

appeared satisfactory, she registered and engaged a comfortable room overlooking the lake.

"I must telephone home," Nancy decided. "If I don't, Laura will be worried to death."

Accordingly, she placed a long distance call to River Heights and after a short wait heard Hannah's voice at the other end of the wire. In response to her request, Laura was called to the telephone. Nancy explained quickly where she was and that she intended to investigate Jacob Aborn's cottage as soon as it grew dark. There was a pause, and then Laura's anxious voice reached her.

"Oh, Nancy, I'm afraid to have you try that."

"I'm sure I've struck a clue, Laura, and it would be foolish of me to come home without investigating."

"Do be careful."

"I will," Nancy promised. "Has father come back from St. Louis yet?"

"No, he hasn't returned."

Nancy was disappointed, for she had wished to ask his advice.

"Then I guess that's all," she told Laura.

"When will you get back to River Heights?"

"I don't know, Laura. It all depends on what I discover. If I don't telephone again within twenty-four hours send the police to Jacob Aborn's bungalow looking for me."

Just then the telephone operator warned
Nancy that her time was up, and she hastily
hung up the receiver. Glancing at her watch
she saw that it was five o'clock.

"At least three hours to wait," Nancy
sighed.

She sank down in a comfortable chair and
attempted to read a magazine, but soon gave it
up. She realized that the adventure before
her was apt to prove a dangerous one. Although unafraid, she was somewhat nervous
and waited impatiently for nightfall.

"I wish I had brought dad's revolver," she
thought. "I may need it before I get through."

It was Nancy's plan to visit Jacob Aborn's
residence on the lake, and, if she had sufficient
time, the deserted bungalow she had accidentally
noticed in the forest. She did not know what
she expected to discover. She knew only that
she was playing a "hunch" and that frequently her swift impressions were correct.

At six o'clock she went downstairs for dinner. As she sat alone at a small table in one
corner of the room, many diners regarded her
with interest, for Nancy Drew was an unusually attractive girl, and the prospect of a
daring adventure had brought a becoming
flush to her cheeks.

Upon leaving the dining room, she loitered
about the veranda for a few minutes, watching

the dancers, gazing at the lake, and enjoying the music of the orchestra. But she soon went to her own room.

The moment it became dark enough for her purpose, she left the hotel and called for her roadster, which she had parked at a garage only a short distance away. Eagerly she set off toward Jacob Aborn's bungalow.

Laura had told her how to reach the house. There were two means of approach, one from the lake road and one through the forest. Nancy selected the latter road, believing it to be more secluded. As she drew near the bungalow, she turned the automobile out of the road and ran it into a clump of bushes where it would not be seen. Switching off the engine and locking the doors, she took her flashlight and set off afoot through the woods toward the lake.

Catching her first glimpse of the bungalow, Nancy was impressed.

"What a beautiful summer home," she thought. "If only Jacob Aborn were different, how happy Laura might have been here."

Continuing through the woods, Nancy cautiously approached the house from the rear. Pausing in the shadow of the trees, she hesitated uncertainly.

"If Jacob Aborn catches me here, there's

no telling what he'd do to me," she thought uneasily.

The windows of the bungalow were dark. That suited Nancy's purpose, for she had no intention of attempting to enter the house if Jacob Aborn were at home. Although courageous, she was not foolhardy.

Now that she had reached the bungalow, Nancy asked herself what course she should follow. She comprehended the risk she must take if she entered the house. Should Jacob Aborn catch her in the act, he would probably cause her arrest. Would it be wise to take the chance?

"I'll try it, anyway," she decided resolutely. "I must help Laura."

With a quick glance about to make sure that there was no one in the vicinity to observe her actions, she darted across the clearing and came to the side door. Gently turning the handle, she found the door locked.

"I'll get in through a window," she thought.

An investigation of several windows on the ground floor revealed that they, too, were securely fastened. Nancy was troubled until she recalled that Laura had told her she had left the window of her room unfastened. From her description, Nancy thought she could locate the room and effect an entrance.

After a complete tour of the house, she paused below a window which she believed must be the one Laura had mentioned. Glancing up, she noticed a rose trellis which reached from the ground to the second floor. Making a critical examination, she decided that it would be strong enough to bear her weight.

As quietly as possible, she climbed the trellis. The fragile structure wobbled and creaked, but did not give way. Slightly out of breath, Nancy Drew reached the window ledge.

Trying the window, she found to her delight that it could be raised easily. She crawled through and switched on her flashlight.

She knew at once that she was in Laura's room, for in her flight the girl had left nearly all of her possessions behind. However, there was no time to look around, for as Nancy tiptoed across the room, she was startled to hear a peculiar noise.

Halting abruptly, she listened. To her ears came the unmistakable sound of a heavy footstep on the stairway. Someone was coming!

Nancy feared that she was trapped. There was not sufficient time for her to climb through the window and descend the trellis. Was it possible that Jacob Aborn was in the house after all? The darkened windows had led her to believe that he was away, and in climbing up the trellis she had not been as quiet as she might have been. Perhaps he was coming to find out the cause of the noise. The thought struck her with terror.

Desperately, she looked around for a hiding place. She saw a closet, and darted toward it. Scarcely had she stepped inside and closed the door, when she heard the footsteps coming toward Laura's room.

Frantically, Nancy Drew switched off her flashlight and crouched in a far corner behind a mass of dresses. Scarcely daring to breathe, she waited.

CHAPTER XIII

A NARROW ESCAPE

As NANCY DREW crouched in the dark closet, she heard the door slam and knew that someone had entered Laura Pendleton's room.

At first, in an agony of suspense, the girl remained motionless in her hiding place, but presently as the closet door was not opened, her curiosity gained the upper hand. Cautiously, she peeped out through the keyhole.

It was Jacob Aborn who had entered. She saw that he had placed an oil lamp on the desk and was busy at Laura's dressing table. Apparently, he had not heard Nancy, for he did not glance toward the closet.

Ruthlessly, the man jerked out drawers from the dressing table and emptied the contents upon the bed. As he surveyed the assortment of bottles and boxes, he gave a disgusted grunt. What was it he was looking for, Nancy wondered.

She was not left in doubt long, for Jacob Aborn muttered to himself:

"Drat that girl! She got away with all of

them jewels! Wait until I get hold of her again!''

His fists clinched, and a vicious, cruel expression settled over his face.

As Nancy Drew gazed upon Jacob Aborn, there was no longer any doubt in her mind as to the character of the man. He was a common thief! It was now clear to her that his sole interest in Laura was to get possession of her property. Only her opportune escape from the house had prevented him from stealing her mother's jewels.

Nancy was frightened by her discovery, for now she realized that she was dealing with a hardened criminal. She dared not think of what might become of her, should he learn that she was spying upon him.

''How did he ever get to be Laura's guardian?'' she asked herself in bewilderment. ''I can't believe that Mrs. Pendleton knew his true character, or she wouldn't have entrusted her daughter to him.''

Her thoughts along that line came to an abrupt end as the man moved toward the closet. Fearfully, Nancy ducked down behind Laura's dresses again and prayed that she would not be discovered.

The closet door was jerked violently open and Jacob Aborn looked in. Nancy held her breath, each minute expecting to be **dragged** from her hiding place.

The man gave the closet only a casual glance and then turned away.

"Bah!" he muttered savagely. "Nothing but clothing! A lot of good that will do me! It's money I want!"

The man was about to close the closet **door** when he came to a sudden pause.

"Might be a good thing to look over some **of** these clothes," he murmured. "She may have left something hidden there. Can't tell what girls are up to these days."

Nancy's heart sank within her because she felt that if the man took down any of the dresses behind which she was hidden she **would** surely be discovered. She hardly dared breathe as she wondered what would happen next.

The man took down the first dress **within** reach and stepped out to examine it in the light. He found nothing in the garment **and** threw it rudely over a chair. Then he came back to the closet.

As he reached in, Nancy felt that discovery was close at hand. She wondered whether she could dash past the man, down the stairs, and get out of the building before he could grab her.

Before he could get hold of the next garment an interruption occurred. There was **a loud** noise downstairs which made both the man and Nancy start in surprise.

"What in thunder was that?" muttered Jacob Aborn. He was evidently much disturbed, and, turning abruptly, he ran out into the hall. Then Nancy heard him going down the stairs.

The girl thought of the window and the rose trellis. Could she make her escape that way during Aborn's absence? Before she could make up her mind she heard the man returning.

"Confound those screens on hinges," she heard him mutter. "That's the second time they've scared me. Bah, I must be getting nervous!"

The trip downstairs had evidently put Jacob Aborn in a worse humor than ever. He walked to the closet and surveyed the remaining dresses in disgust.

"Guess I won't bother with them," the girl heard him remark.

Slamming the door, he turned and walked over to the desk. As Nancy again peered out through the keyhole she felt a trifle weak from the fright she had experienced.

"That was a narrow escape," she told herself. "I thought the jig was up."

Unaware that he was being watched, Jacob Aborn began pawing over the papers which were in the desk. Picking up a package of let-

ters, he scanned them hastily and contemptu-
ously tossed them upon the floor.

It was with difficulty that Nancy controlled
her anger as she saw the man read Laura's
private correspondence. She longed to fly out
at him and accuse him face to face. However,
she was far too wise to allow herself to be
governed by a mad impulse. She must bide her
time.

After a few minutes, her limbs became
cramped, and she shifted her position. To her
horror, a board creaked underfoot. Nancy felt
that all was lost as she again ducked behind
the dresses.

Jacob Aborn heard the noise and wheeled
about. He walked toward the closet. Halfway across the room he paused and laughed
shortly.

"Couldn't have been anything," he muttered. "Just looked in that closet not more
than a minute ago."

Without troubling himself to pick up the
articles he had scattered over the floor, the man
took the lamp and left the room. In relief,
Nancy Drew stepped from her hiding place.

"I suppose I'd better skip while I can," she
advised herself.

She tiptoed across the room to the window,
but did not open it. Instead she stood lost in
deep thought. Although Nancy realized full

well the danger of remaining longer in the house, she had the instincts of a detective. So long as there was a chance that she might learn more by waiting, she hesitated to leave.

She could hear Jacob Aborn descending the stairs to the first floor.

"I'll not leave yet," she decided firmly.

Softly opening the door, she crept down the carpeted hall. After listening a minute, she quietly slipped down the stairway, taking care not to step in the middle of the boards lest they squeak and betray her presence.

Reaching the living room, she paused to listen. She could hear Jacob Aborn moving about in the kitchen. Overcome by curiosity, she tiptoed to the door.

"If only some errand would take him outside," she thought hopefully.

Her wish was gratified, for presently the man picked up a water bucket and left the house. Taking advantage of the opportunity, Nancy darted into the kitchen and hid in the broom closet. She marveled at her own bravery, for she knew that she was taking a great risk. Nevertheless, she was determined to discover what Jacob Aborn was about.

In a few minutes the man returned with the bucket of water. To Nancy's disappointment he picked up a basket of groceries on the table and began to prepare his supper.

The air in the closet became unpleasantly warm and close, and she began to regret that she had sought the hiding place. However, her interest quickened as she saw Laura's guardian wrap up a number of sandwiches, an orange, and an apple in a newspaper.

"There, that's ready for to-morrow," she heard him mutter.

Placing the bundle on the kitchen table, the man sat down and began to eat his supper.

In fascination, Nancy stared at the bundle on the table. What could it mean? She recalled that Laura had told her she had frequently seen her guardian leave the house with a small package. Did Jacob Aborn always carry food in the bundle? If so, what became of it?

Nancy Drew was puzzled, and the more she tried to think of an explanation, the more bewildered she became. Certainly, she had stumbled upon a mystery.

"That man was carrying a bundle to-day when I saw him walking through the forest," she reasoned. "Then when he caught me looking through the window of the deserted bungalow, the bundle was gone. I believe it will be worth my while to have another look at that bungalow!"

Now that she had stumbled upon what she considered a valuable clue, Nancy Drew was eager to get away from the house. But so long as Jacob Aborn remained in the kitchen, she was held a prisoner.

Impatiently, she watched him eat his supper, and it seemed to her that he would never get through. Even after he had finished, he leaned back in his chair and studied the floor meditatively. The expression upon his face was not pleasant to behold.

"I'll venture he's cooking up some dirty scheme," Nancy told herself.

At last the man pushed back his chair and picked up the oil lamp.

"May as well get busy," he grunted. "I've got a big night before me."

Leaving the bundle upon the table, he turned and left the kitchen. A few minutes later, Nancy heard him trudging heavily up the staircase.

"Now what shall I do?" she asked herself in perplexity, as she came out of the closet.

Escape was a simple matter, for the kitchen door had been left unlocked. However, Nancy was not altogether certain that she wished to leave the house so soon. Jacob Aborn's last statement held her interest.

What did he mean by, "a big night before him"? Was he planning more mischief? Nancy Drew determined to wait and find out.

CHAPTER XIV

STARTLING REVELATIONS

STEALING quietly into the living room, Nancy Drew paused at the foot of the stairway. Although eager to find out what Jacob Aborn was doing on the floor above, she told herself that it would be rash to follow him there. While she was debating what to do, she heard a creaking of boards and realized that the man was coming back.

Hastily ducking down out of sight behind the davenport, she waited. She was no longer afraid she would be discovered, for she had noticed that Jacob Aborn was too absorbed in his own plans to be observant. If she kept perfectly quiet she did not believe that she would be detected.

The man came slowly down the stairs, dragging two heavy suitcases. Dropping them upon the living-room floor, he opened the lids and surveyed the contents critically.

His back was to the davenport, and Nancy daringly peeped out. She saw that the suitcases were packed with wearing apparel. However, it was not the clothing, but rather a gruesome object on top of one of the bags that held her attention. Jacob Aborn carried a weapon, and a wicked looking one at that! Nancy Drew shuddered and almost regretted that she had not escaped when it was possible.

Fastening down the covers of the luggage, Jacob Aborn locked the suitcases and strapped them.

"There, that job is done," he muttered when he had finished. "Nothing like being prepared. They'll never catch Stumpy asleep!"

The name burned itself into Nancy Drew's brain. Stumpy! What could it mean? He had called himself by a name which was suggestive of the underworld. As Nancy stared at him she became convinced that he was a professional crook. Laura was indeed under the control of a dangerous guardian!

Her reflections were cut short when Jacob Aborn placed the suitcases against the wall and turned toward a small safe in one corner of the room. In amazement, Nancy watched him work at the dial. After he had made several unsuccessful attempts to open the door, it finally swung open.

With a grunt of satisfaction, the man removed several packages of bank bills. His eyes became greedy and gloating as he gazed upon the money.

Nancy had no way of telling the denomination of the bills, but she felt certain that Jacob Aborn held a small fortune in his hands. Where had he secured the money and what did he mean to do with it?

"I may as well leave it here until to-morrow," the man grunted.

He placed the neat packages of money back in the safe and, closing the heavy door, turned the dial. Then with a tired yawn, he moved toward the stairway.

"Guess I'll turn in. Got to be up early to-morrow."

He climbed the stairs, carrying the light with him. Nancy heard him enter a bedroom and slam the door. Soon the house became quiet.

Slipping noiselessly from her hiding place, Nancy Drew tiptoed toward the kitchen. Due to an oversight, the back door had been left unlocked and opened readily. With a sigh of relief that she at last had escaped unharmed from the house, Nancy stepped out into the night.

It was very dark, for there was no moon. She crossed the clearing and rapidly set off through the forest, using her flashlight to guide her steps.

Her adventures were beginning to tire her

and before she knew it she took a wrong path
and presently brought up in the midst of some
bushes and rocks.

"My gracious, this isn't right!" she told herself. "Why, I really believe I've lost myself."

She turned the flashlight downward and saw
before her a spring of water. A tin cup was
on a near-by rock.

"Well, anyway, here's where I can get a
drink," she told herself. "And goodness knows
I'm thirsty enough."

The water was clear and cool and the drink
refreshed Nancy very much. Placing the cup
where she had found it, she retraced her steps
and after a few minutes of walking found the
spot where she had gone wrong. With more
care she set off through the forest. It was
dark and silent, and she could not repress a
feeling of intense loneliness as she proceeded.

A few minutes later she reached the roadster
which she had hidden behind a clump of bushes.
As she climbed in and sank back against the
cushions, she considered her next move. Until now, she had had no time to work out a plan
of action.

Of one thing she was certain. Jacob Aborn
was a criminal. She was convinced that he intended to run away from Melrose Lake, for
otherwise he would not have packed his suitcases. Undoubtedly, he intended to take the

money which was in the safe with him. Nancy
had no proof that it did not belong to him, but
in her mind there was a growing suspicion that
he might have stolen it from Laura Pendleton's
estate.

"At least he won't try to get away to-night,"
she reasoned, "because he's gone to bed. And
he said something about needing that bundle
of food to-morrow."

Nancy was at a loss to know what to do next.
Although convinced that Jacob Aborn was a
criminal, she was well aware that she had no
evidence against him.   In court it would
merely be her word against his, and if it came
to that, she would be embarrassed to explain
her presence in the house.

"I must get definite proof," she thought.

Groping for an idea, she again thought of
the old bungalow in the woods.

"I'm sure it has some connection with the
mystery," she reasoned. "While Jacob Aborn
is out of the way, I'll do a little sleuthing."

To think was to act with Nancy Drew, and
it required but a few minutes for her to drive
the distance from Jacob Aborn's residence to
the deserted bungalow. Although the night was
dark, she found the side road without difficulty.

Halting the car in the bushes, she picked up

her flashlight and started toward the bungalow. Not without misgiving, she pushed
through the forest.

"I hope my flashlight doesn't play out," she
worried. "I'll never find the bungalow if it
does."

There was no path leading through the
woods, but Nancy was fairly certain of her directions. Soon she stepped out into a tiny
clearing, and, directly ahead, saw the old
bungalow.

Hurrying across the open space, she paused
in front of the building. It was dark and silent,
but as she gazed upon it an uneasy feeling took
possession of her. Her inner self seemed to
warn her not to enter the bungalow.

"This is no time to hesitate," she told herself sternly. "If Jacob Aborn is to be caught,
I must gather my evidence to-night. To-
morrow he may skip out."

As Nancy moved toward the rear of the
bungalow, she glanced down at her flashlight
and was alarmed to see that it was beginning
to grow dim.

"Just my luck to have it go out when I need
it the most!" she thought in disgust.

In an attempt to save the battery, she
switched off the light. As her eyes became accustomed to the dark, she was able to see a

little. Nancy was determined to effect an entrance, but just how it could be accomplished she did not know.

A tour of the bungalow revealed that all of the doors were locked. This she had expected. The boards had fallen from one of the windows —the one through which she had peered that afternoon when surprised by Laura's guardian. However, the window was high above her head, and even if she stood on a box, she doubted that she could raise herself to the ledge.

Undaunted, she examined the other windows, and on the south side of the bungalow found one which opened from a porch. It was boarded up, and her efforts to dislodge the barrier were futile.

Resistance only whetted Nancy Drew's desire to enter the bungalow, and at once she began searching the yard for something with which to pry. After an unsuccessful hunt, she was forced to switch on her flashlight for a few minutes, until she found a stout stick which would serve her purpose.

Wedging it in between the boards, she pried with all her might. For a moment, the first board offered stubborn resistance, and then, with a groan and a squeak, gave way. The remaining boards were removed with less difficulty.

To Nancy's joy, the window was unlocked.

Pushing it up, she peered into the living room. It was dark and she could see nothing.

"Well, here's for it!" she decided fatalistically.

Halfway through the window, she hesitated without knowing just why she did it. Nervously, she glanced back over her shoulder. A queer sensation passed over her, leaving her a trifle frightened. She felt exactly as though someone were following her.

"How silly!" she scolded herself.

Nevertheless, she turned searching eyes toward the forest. So far as she could see there was no one in sight. Nancy listened intently, but all that she heard was the whispering of the wind in the maple trees.

"Nerves," she decided firmly. "Jacob Aborn won't bother me to-night. He's probably asleep at this minute."

She swung herself through the window and switched on her flashlight. She stood in the living room, or such she judged it to be, for it was bare of furniture.

"Nothing here!" Nancy told herself.

Hastily she moved toward the next room. Her light was gradually growing dimmer, and she knew that she must work quickly unless she wished to be left in total darkness.

She entered a smaller room. Flashing the beam of her light over the walls and floor, she was disappointed to find nothing of interest.

Nancy was sorely perplexed. In visiting the deserted bungalow she had "played a hunch," and now it seemed that she had made a mistake.

"I haven't seen it all yet," she encouraged herself.

Then her light revealed a small door, and she moved curiously over toward it. Halfway across the room, an unusual sound arrested her attention. Had she heard a board creak behind her or was it only imagination?

After hesitating a second, Nancy Drew again started toward the door. As she reached out to grasp the knob, her body became tense.

This time there was no mistake. She heard a peculiar sound which seemed to come from the floor.

"It sounded like a groan," was the thought which flashed through her mind.

Was it possible that someone was imprisoned in the cellar? The fear that some person was in distress gave her the courage to open the door.

As it swung back, she saw before her a long flight of stone stairs leading down into darkness. A gust of cold, musty air struck her in the face and momentarily repulsed her.

Nancy glanced nervously at her flashlight. She told herself that the battery could not last

much longer. Already the light was so dim
that she could barely see the steps in front of
her. Should she investigate the cellar? She
had no idea what it might reveal, and the
thought of being caught below without a light
sent a cold shiver over her.

Yet, Nancy felt that she was about to stumble
upon the real secret of the old bungalow, and
the thrill of anticipated victory urged her forward. Cautiously, she descended the steps, one
at a time.

She came to a sharp turn and peered anxiously down into the black abyss.

To her horror she saw a man stretched out
full length upon a bench directly below her.
His face was turned upward and Nancy caught
a full glimpse of the countenance.

It was Jacob Aborn!

CHAPTER XV

A Familiar Face

For an instant, Nancy Drew was spellbound. Her eyes dilated with fear, she stood like a stone image, gazing down into the face of Jacob Aborn.

How had the rascal reached the bungalow ahead of her? What was he doing in the cellar? A dozen questions flashed through her mind, but the one which troubled her the most was whether or not the man had seen her.

As Nancy was held in a paralysis of fear, the light in her flashlight flickered again. Then, it went out, leaving her in total darkness.

Sheer panic took possession of Nancy. Turning, she gave a low cry and stumbled up the stairway. Jerking open the door at the top, she ran through the room. Her flight was abruptly checked as she crashed into a table.

Reaching out to catch herself from falling, Nancy's hand touched an object. Eagerly, she felt of it and discovered that it was a lantern. Snatching it up, she stumbled on.

Coming to a door she pulled it open. To her chagrin she ran into a wall. She had entered a closet.

Frantically, she rushed out again, and found another door to the left. She had made no mistake this time, and to her relief found herself in the living room. In desperate haste she reached the window, and, climbing through, leaped to the porch.

Fully expecting to hear a shot behind her, she ran as fast as she could across the clearing to the forest.

Breathless, she reached the shelter of the trees and paused to look back. To her astonishment she was not being followed. Jacob Aborn was nowhere in sight. The old bungalow appeared as deserted and silent as before.

"That's queer," she told herself. "Perhaps he didn't see me after all."

A moment's serious consideration convinced her that this reasoning was not logical, for she had made a great deal of noise clattering up the steps. It was inconceivable that he had not heard her when she stumbled into the table, nearly overturning it.

"I don't believe I imagined it," she thought in perplexity. "I'm sure it was Jacob Aborn I saw in that cellar. But how did he get here ahead of me?"

She gravely reflected for a minute. Laura's

guardian had retired to his bedroom before she had slipped from the house. Presumably, she had left him sound asleep. How could he have dressed and reached the bungalow so quickly?

"I wonder if it could have been Jacob Aborn," she mused. "After I left his house I didn't waste a minute. I came directly here in the roadster. He couldn't have beaten me to it unless he flew!"

For several minutes, Nancy Drew stood in the shadows of the trees watching the bungalow. After considerable time had elapsed and still no one appeared, she began to grow curious as well as impatient.

"I know there was someone in that cellar," she assured herself, "and I'd like to find out who it is. If I only had a light, I'd be tempted to go back."

As the daring thought occurred to her, she glanced down and noticed that she was still clutching the lantern which she had snatched from the table as she ran. She had picked it up purely on impulse, without thinking that she might use it later. Now she decided that it would serve a useful purpose. There was only one drawback—it was not lighted.

"A lot of good it will do me without a match," she murmured in disgust.

As she stood staring gloomily at the lantern,

she feared that she must admit defeat. Brave as she was, she hesitated to return to the bungalow without a light to guide her. If only she had brought an extra flashlight battery with her! Or her father's revolver!

"I wouldn't be afraid if I had some way to protect myself," she told herself. "Or if I could see where I was going."

As she stood gazing moodily at the old, deserted house, a thought came to her. Eagerly she began to search through her pockets. To her delight, after thrusting her hand into the last pocket, she brought out a small box of matches. She had used the matches while in camp at Moon Lake, keeping them in a waterproof container for an emergency. She had carelessly left them in her dress pocket, and upon returning home had forgotten all about them. For once her negligence had been to her advantage.

Hastily opening the box, she found several matches left. Examining the lantern, she was encouraged to discover that it was nearly full of oil. Striking a match upon a stone, she applied it to the wick.

Before the wick ignited, a mischievous gust of wind extinguished the flame. Nancy tried again, and to her disgust, the second match met a similar fate.

In alarm she felt in the box. There was only

one match left. If she failed in her next attempt she would be without a light.

Stepping back into the forest so that the wind would not strike her, she hopefully struck the last match. As the flame spurted up, she applied it to the lantern and was gratified to see it ignite the wick.

"I'd better cover the lantern while I cross the clearing," she advised herself. "I don't want to make myself a gun target."

Stripping off her sweater, she wrapped it around the lantern, and then set off toward the bungalow. As she stole cautiously forward she frequently paused to listen. No unusual sound disturbed the tranquillity of the night. The old bungalow was as quiet as a tomb.

The queer place looked unusually queer at this hour of the night, and it was no wonder that Nancy paused as she gazed upon it.

"There's some terrible mystery here—I'm sure of it," she breathed to herself. "I've got to be careful. I don't want to be caught napping."

The girl looked around her in all directions. No one was in sight and not a sound disturbed the silence.

For one brief instant as she drew closer to the building Nancy had an inclination to turn and flee. Then she braced herself.

"I won't do it!" she told herself. "I came here to find out what all this means and I'm going to do it. Nancy Drew, don't be a goose. This isn't half as bad as things were at the Turnbull mansion. And remember what you went through with to get the old clock!" and she braced up once more.

After a slight hesitation, Nancy Drew crept up on the porch. For the second time that evening she experienced an uneasy sensation. It was not so much the fear that she was running into danger as it was a feeling that she was being followed.

Boldly, she thrust her head and shoulders through the window. Nothing but an oppressive silence greeted her.

"Have I been dreaming?" Nancy thought in perplexity. "Is it possible there's no one in the bungalow after all?"

Somewhat impatient at herself, she placed the lantern upon the floor and climbed through the window. Picking up the light, she flashed it about the room. Reassured, she tiptoed forward.

A board creaked underfoot, and she paused nervously. Then from below she heard a peculiar noise. It sounded like a moan of pain.

Startled, Nancy Drew held herself rigid, scarcely daring to move a muscle. As she listened she heard the sound again. This time she knew there was no mistake. Someone had groaned.

"Oh, what shall I do?" she asked herself nervously. "Who can it be?"

At that moment a pitiful cry arose from the floor below.

"Help!"

Nancy opened her lips, but no sound issued forth. She tried again, and scarcely recognized her own voice.

"Who's there?" she demanded shakily.

The only response was another feeble call. "Help! Help!"

The cry echoed through the deserted bungalow, ending in a plaintive wail. Then the house became silent.

CHAPTER XVI

WHAT NANCY DISCOVERED

WHEN Nancy Drew heard the cry for help, she no longer considered her own safety. The thought that someone might be in pain drove her to action. Summoning all her courage, she hurried to the cellar door and opened it.

Reaching the first landing, she stood listening quietly. The scratchy rustling of a mouse in a wall near by caused her to catch her breath.

"Why, it's only a mouse," she told herself. "I'm certainly not going to let that scare me."

Nevertheless she came to a standstill and did not attempt to move again until the sounds made by the mouse had died away entirely. Then she braced herself once more.

She took a step forward, holding the lantern before her. Cautiously, she crept down the first stair step and then paused again. She wondered what awaited her in the depths of the dark cellar below.

Then there came to her ears a faint metallic clank. It seemed to proceed from below and she was at a loss to understand what it could have been. There it was again!

But this time it came as a series of metallic sounds, and Nancy realized that she was listening to the clanking of chains. "Was it possible that someone was confined below in fetters?" she asked herself. Then another thought came to her—perhaps a vicious dog was chained in the cellar, ready to throw itself upon any intruder.

Almost at once Nancy dismissed the fear. If it were a dog, she told herself, it would have growled at her first approach. Thus reassured, she held the lantern before her and slowly descended the stairs, peering anxiously into the murky darkness.

Turning the light upon the spot where she had seen the man on her previous excursion into the cellar, she beheld a disheveled human being lying on a bench against the side of the stone wall.

Nancy started backward, and the lantern wavered in her hand. She was almost sure that the man before her was Jacob Aborn. Tempted to run away, she overcame the impulse and again peered critically down at the white face which was turned toward her.

"It isn't Jacob Aborn," she decided, "but there's a startling resemblance."

No longer afraid, Nancy Drew rapidly descended the stairs to the cellar. With a cry of pity, she ran toward the man who lay so white and still on the bench.

At a glance she took in the scene before her. In reality the cellar was a dungeon, for the walls were of solid stone and there were no windows. Not a ray of light filtered into the horrible place.

The room was damp and musty, and as she accidentally brushed against a wall it felt clammy and cold to the touch. A heavy chain was fastened to the wall above the bench. To Nancy's horror the end of the chain was attached to the prisoner in such a way that it allowed him some freedom of motion and yet held him a captive.

"Oh!" Nancy cried as she gazed upon the imprisoned man.

The prisoner did not stir. He lay perfectly still upon the bench.

"Oh, he can't be dead," Nancy whispered fearfully.

Dropping down on her knees, she felt of the man's pulse. It was faint, but regular.

"He's just unconscious," she thought in relief. "The strain of realizing help was near must have been too much for him."

She fell to work chafing his wrists, and for the first time noticed the cruel crimson marks which had been caused by the chains.

"I wonder what fiend is responsible for this?" she asked herself angrily.

Now that she gazed directly into the man's face, she wondered how she could have mistaken him for Jacob Aborn. To be sure, the two men were of the same build, although the prisoner appeared gaunt and thin as though he had not been properly fed during his captivity. Their features were similar also. But while Jacob Aborn's face was characterized by harsh lines, the prisoner had a gentle, kind expression.

Nancy Drew did not further concern herself with the man's appearance, for she was alarmed that he did not recover consciousness.

"I must do something!" she thought desperately. "Perhaps I can find some water——"

Catching up the lantern, she mounted the stairs two at a time. Reaching the kitchen, she was overjoyed to see a pump at the sink.

After a search through the cupboards she at last found a leaky tin vessel which would serve her purpose. Quickly filling it, she rushed back to the cellar.

Wetting her handkerchief, she applied it gently to the prisoner's forehead. When he did not revive, she sprinkled a little of the water on his face.

The man stirred slightly and moaned. Encouraged, Nancy again soaked her handkerchief and applied it to his head. She saw that he was regaining consciousness.

Then the prisoner's body twitched violently, and his eyes fluttered open.

"Help!" he called feebly.

Nancy saw that the man was delirious.

"Help has come," she said gently. "Don't try to struggle. You are in the hands of a friend."

"Friend?" the man asked stupidly.

As he attempted to raise himself to a sitting position, Nancy helped him.

"Didn't think—help—ever come," he murmured weakly.

His eyes, which were bright with fever, fastened upon the pan Nancy held in her hand.

"Water," he begged thickly.

Nancy handed over the basin with alacrity and the man drank greedily.

"First I've had to drink in twenty-four hours," he said more steadily.

He stared at Nancy as though he had not seen her before.

"How did you get here?" he demanded.

"I heard your cries for help."

"Oh, yes, I remember now. I heard someone coming and I called out. That was the last I remembered."

"Who are you?" Nancy questioned. "Why are you in chains?"

A bitter expression passed over the prisoner's face.

"I am here through the trickery of Stumpy Dowd, a notorious criminal."

"And your name?" Nancy gasped.

"Jacob Aborn."

"Jacob Aborn?" she echoed. "Then——"

"That rascal, Stumpy Dowd is impersonating me," Jacob Aborn finished for her.

"I don't understand."

"I don't wonder at that, Miss——" he groped for a name.

"Drew," Nancy supplied.

"I'm only beginning to comprehend the trick that was played on me by that scamp. And poor Laura! Heaven knows where she is at this moment!"

"She's safe. I left her at my home in River Heights."

"I'm thankful for that! It nearly killed me to think that she might be in the hands of that crook!"

"Tell me the entire story," Nancy begged. "What do you know about Stumpy Dowd?"

"I know enough to send him to prison for the rest of his life! He's a fraud. This isn't the first deal he's been mixed up in. He's trying to get his hands on Laura Pendleton's fortune. I'm afraid he has everything by this time."

Jacob Aborn buried his hands in his face.

"How did Stumpy get you here?" Nancy questioned.

"One night about two weeks ago he came to my house, the bungalow on the lake, on the pretense of seeing me about a business matter."

"Then you own that house that Stumpy is living in!" Nancy interrupted.

"Yes, I thought it would make a nice home for Laura. Well, Stumpy came to see me and as soon as he began to ask questions about the Pendleton estate I was suspicious. Finally, I ordered him from the house. He drew a gun on me."

"And there was no one to help you?"

"No. I had intended to leave for Moon Lake the following day and had given the servants a vacation. I was alone in the house. I put up a fight, but when I was semi-conscious from a blow on the head that scoundrel forced me into this deserted bungalow."

"You haven't been here for two weeks?"

Jacob Aborn nodded grimly.

"Two long weeks. I've nearly gone mad. Chained to this bench like a felon!" With a despairing gesture, he lifted his arms, and his fetters clanked against the floor.

"How horrible!"

"Stumpy Dowd is a fiend! Not content with chaining me here, he's half starved me. If you hadn't come, I couldn't have stood it many more days. Only the thought of Laura has kept me alive. You say she is safe?"

"Yes, she ran away from Stumpy."

"Her property? What has become of it?"

"I don't know," Nancy was forced to admit. "She brought nothing with her except some of her mother's jewels."

"Then Stumpy Dowd must have his hand on every dollar of the fortune," the man groaned. "A rich haul it will make too."

"Laura is wealthy?"

"Yes, her mother left her a sufficient fortune."

"I can't understand why Stumpy remained near here after he secured the property," Nancy commented.

"There are two reasons. First, nearly all of Laura's property was tied up in stocks and bonds—gilt edge of course. Stumpy was forced to impersonate me long enough to convert the securities into cash. At least that's what I suspect."

Nancy nodded thoughtfully.

"And the second reason. I've led him to believe that he hasn't secured all of Laura's property. Stumpy is greedy, and it's his nature to get his hands on everything. He has tried to force me to tell what became of the remaining securities."

"You wouldn't tell?"

"I couldn't if I wished."

"Then he has everything in his possession now, has he?"

"Everything except the jewels. How can I ever face Laura again?"

"Don't think about that," Nancy returned quickly. "It wasn't your fault. Stumpy Dowd is a very clever crook, but he won't get away this time!"

"Is he still at Melrose Lake?" Jacob Aborn asked eagerly. "If we could only capture him——"

"Rest assured, we will. But we must work quickly. I happen to know that he is planning his escape. I think he intends to get away to-morrow. He has Laura's money in the safe."

"Then if we can set the police on him to-night we'll save the fortune!"

"Exactly! But first we must get away from here."

With troubled eyes, Nancy Drew gazed at the chain which held Laura Pendleton's guardian a prisoner.

"If only I can break the chain!"

"It isn't necessary. I know where Stumpy keeps the key to the padlock."

"Where?"

"Hanging on a hook in the stairway."

"I'll get it!" Nancy cried eagerly.

Turning, she hastened toward the stairs. Had she not been so intent upon setting Jacob Aborn free she might have heard a peculiar rustling sound from the direction of the kitchen. Oblivious of possible danger, she rushed up the steps two at a time. In her haste she had forgotten the lantern and was forced to return for it.

Snatching it up from the floor, she again started toward the stairs, turning her head to call back an encouragement to the prisoner.

"We'll soon have you out of here, Mr. Aborn."

"Hurry!" the man urged. "We have waited too long now."

Nancy was of the same opinion, for she realized that they must work swiftly if they were to prevent Stumpy's escape. Already it must be long past midnight, and at dawn he would probably leave.

Anxiously, she moved the lantern up and down, illuminating the dingy walls of the staircase. Just above her head to the left she saw the hook for which she was searching. The precious key dangled from it. Snatching it up, she turned and ran down the steps.

"You found it?" Jacob Aborn demanded anxiously.

"Yes, here it is!" Nancy held up the object. "I'll have you free in another minute."

Dropping down upon her knees before the bench, she began to work frantically at the padlock, Mr. Aborn watching her hopefully. So engrossed were they both, that they failed to notice a dark figure creeping slowly down the stairway. Nearer and nearer he came, an ugly revolver gripped tightly in his right hand.

Suddenly Jacob Aborn glanced up and a look of horror froze upon his face.

"Look out!" he shouted.

CHAPTER XVII

A Desperate Situation

THE warning came too late.

Before Nancy Drew could turn, the butt of a revolver crashed down upon her head. With a low moan of pain, she sagged to the floor and lay still.

How long she remained unconscious, she did not know, but when at last she opened her eyes she found herself stretched out on the cold floor of the cellar. She was bewildered and for a minute could not account for the splitting pain in her head.

Then with a shudder she remembered what had happened. She had been struck down from behind. Who was her assailant?

Nancy became aware that someone was standing over her, but objects whirled before her eyes and she could not distinguish the face. Then, abruptly, her vision cleared. She saw Stumpy Dowd gazing down upon her gloatingly.

"You!" she gasped.

The man leered unpleasantly.

"Thought you were going to catch me, did
you? Well, you have another thought coming
this time!"

He reached over, and, catching her by the
arm, jerked her roughly to her feet. Nancy
was so weak that she nearly fell.

"What are you going to do?" she whispered.

"You'll find out soon enough," Stumpy
sneered, as he held up a long rope. "I'm going
to tie you up and leave you here. You and
your friend have so much to say to each other!"

"Let that girl go," Jacob Aborn pleaded
from the other side of the room. "Do anything
you like to me, but set her free."

"Shut up!" Stumpy growled. "I'll do
plenty to both of you before I get through!"

Nancy was too weak to struggle, and she was
aware that resistance would be useless. One
glance at the murderous weapon in Stumpy's
hand had convinced her of that. He was ruth-
less and unprincipled, and would think nothing
of shooting her down if she made a break for
the stairway.

Yet, as Stumpy began to tie her feet together
with the stout rope, she realized she must do
something. If only her head would stop throb-
bing so that she could think clearly! The situation was a desperate one. Unless she thought
quickly there would be no escape.

Then, suddenly, an idea came to her. She

recalled that a detective who had called on her father only a few months before had entertained them by telling of his various experiences with criminals. He had explained how it was possible to hold one's hands while being bound, so as to slip the bonds later. Nancy had been interested, and had pressed the detective for details. He had taken a stout piece of cord and had given her a demonstration. At the time she had thought the trick a very clever one. Little dreaming that the knowledge would ever prove useful, she had made no effort to remember how the hands must be held. Now, she frantically tried to recall what the detective had told her. If only the trick would work!

Holding her wrists in what she believed was the correct position, she permitted Stumpy to bind them securely. The ropes cut into her flesh cruelly. It seemed to her that she must have made a mistake, for certainly there was little space between her wrists and the bonds.

"And now, just to make sure you won't get away—" Stumpy muttered evilly.

He took the end of the rope and ran it through a ring in the wall, knotting it fast.

"I guess that will hold you for a while," he leered.

"You beast!" Nancy cried.

She realized now what Stumpy intended to do, but she was too proud to beg for mercy.

"This will teach you not to meddle in affairs that are none of your business!"

"You'll pay for this!" Jacob Aborn cried in a quavering voice. "If I get free——"

"If you get free! That's good!" Stumpy laughed harshly. Then a cruel look settled over his face and his eyes narrowed. "Why, you old fool, you'll stay here until the rats get you!"

"This isn't the time of the inquisition!" Nancy declared fiercely. "You can't get away with murder!"

"Murder? Who said anything about murder? What a harsh word! I'll just leave you and your friend here and go away. If anything happens——" Dowd shrugged his shoulders indifferently.

"The police will be after you in a day!" Jacob Aborn cried.

"Oh, no they won't. Stumpy is nobody's fool. I'll cover up my trail."

"You think you will," Nancy informed him. "Every criminal thinks he'll escape."

"And I will too," Stumpy boasted. "I'm too clever to be caught. Oh, I guess I've put over my little scheme pretty slick. Not a person suspected that I wasn't the real Jacob Aborn."

"Then you admit your guilt?" Nancy demanded.

Stumpy regarded her appraisingly.

"You're a smart detective, but your smartness won't do you any good this time! I don't mind admitting I pulled the deal single handed, because you'll never get out of here to squeal on me.''

As neither Jacob Aborn or Nancy Drew made a response, he continued boastingly.

"I'm all fixed for my get-away to-night. Would have waited until to-morrow if you hadn't come nosing into my business." He glared at Nancy. "I've cashed in all the Pendleton property, and my suitcases are packed. When I leave here, I'll get them and beat it in a new racing car I bought to-day. I'd like to see the police or anyone catch me, once I get started!"

"You'll pay for it some day!" Jacob Aborn cried angrily. "Robbing an orphan! I'm thankful poor Laura is out of your clutches."

"Oh, you think she is, do you?" Stumpy laughed evilly. "Well, let me tell you I know where she's hiding."

A look of horror came into Mr. Aborn's eyes, for his one consolation had been the thought that his ward was safe.

"I heard you two talking," Stumpy informed them. "I found out she's in River Heights, and I'm going there to-night!"

"Don't you dare harm Laura Pendleton!"

In spite of his condition, Jacob Aborn struggled in his chains, attempting to attack Stumpy.

With one blow, the scoundrel sent him reeling against the wall.

"I don't care what becomes of that ward of yours," he snarled. "It's the jewels I want. I'll fix Laura for sneaking away with them."

"If you try to kidnap Laura you'll have my father to deal with," Nancy promised. "He's a criminal lawyer!"

"A criminal lawyer, eh? Well, I may take a shot at him just for luck."

As Stumpy spoke, he caught sight of an object on the floor. It was the key to the padlock on Aborn's chains. When Nancy had fallen, it had slipped from her hand.

"Well, I'll just take it with me," he announced gleefully, as he picked it up.

As he was about to thrust it into his pocket, another thought came to him. He hung it on a nail, far out of the reach of the two prisoners.

"You can look at it until you rot," he told them.

Turning, he started to leave the cellar. Halfway across the room, he came back and stood gloating down upon Nancy.

"You thought you were so clever, sneaking into my house and spying on me. You the daughter of a brilliant lawyer! Well, let me tell you something—you overlooked one important detail."

Nancy stared blankly at Stumpy. She was

at a loss to know how she had given herself away.

"The next time you'll remember to muffle the engine of your automobile when you leave!" He gave a hollow laugh which echoed through the place. "The next time!"

"You fiend!" Jacob said fiercely.

"Thank you for the compliment," Stumpy made an elaborate bow. "And now, I fear I must say good-bye. Too bad you can't come with me. I shall live high in some other country."

With another mocking bow, he turned and left the two prisoners. They heard him stumble up the stairway and slam the door at the top.

CHAPTER XVIII

LEFT TO STARVE

A DEATHLIKE quiet fell upon the old bungalow. Nancy Drew and Jacob Aborn stared at each other in despair. Stumpy Dowd had dared to carry out his threat. He had left them in the cellar to starve.

Fastened to the wall at opposite sides of the room, they were unable to help each other. Aborn's bonds were such that he could move about, but his tether was too short to permit him to reach Nancy, who lay on the floor, bound hand and foot. Their situation seemed hopeless.

In his haste, Stumpy Down had forgotten the lantern, and now its dim light served to reveal the sordidness of the prison. In a short time the oil would burn out and then they would be left in the dark—a darkness which would soon drive them mad.

However, Nancy Drew's first thought was not for herself, but for Laura. She recalled Stumpy's threat, and was afraid that he would go to River Heights and attempt to harm the girl.

"I hope dad is home from St. Louis," she thought miserably. "He'll look after her."

At the best, she knew that Laura would be left penniless. Even now Stumpy was making his escape with the Pendleton fortune. After going to River Heights he would undoubtedly strike for the border. Once in a foreign country he would enjoy his ill-gotten gains in comparative safety.

The same thought was passing through the mind of Jacob Aborn, for in desperation he sprang up from the bench and paced the floor like a caged lion. He shook his chains and beat them wildly against the stone wall until his wrists were cut and bleeding.

"If I could only get my hands on that wretch!" he cried bitterly.

Again he clawed at his chains, but could not break them. In vain he pounded the padlock against the floor. Not until he was completely exhausted did he give up. Then he quietly collapsed on the bench.

"Oh, my poor Laura," he half sobbed. "And to think that I promised her mother I'd always look after her."

Nancy gazed upon the man in compassion, but could think of nothing to say in comfort. The situation seemed unreal to her. She felt that it was a horrible nightmare, from which she must soon awaken.

However, the dull ache in her head and the cutting ropes were severe reminders of her plight. If only she could find a means of escape!

She considered shouting for help, but almost at once decided that it would only be a waste of energy. The bungalow was located in a desolate portion of the forest and seldom did anyone pass near the spot. Jacob Aborn had been held a prisoner for nearly two weeks, and had been unable to make his cries heard.

It was characteristic of Nancy Drew to keep her head when faced with a grave problem. Stumpy Dowd had left her to die, but the will to live was strong within her. She would not give up without a brave struggle.

"If only I can free my hands!" she thought grimly.

She glanced down at the ropes meditatively. To the eye there was no space between the thongs and her wrists, and yet if she had made no mistake, she should be able to move her hands in such a way that she could slip out of the ropes. If only the trick would work!

Giving her wrists a peculiar twist, she was elated to find a little slack in the ropes. She tried to slip her hands from the bonds but could not. However, Nancy was not ready to give up. She hoped that by moving her hands back and forth, she would eventually be able to free herself.

Frantically she began working at the ropes. After a few minutes, her wrists became chafed and tender, but the knowledge that she was making a little progress gave her new courage.

After a time, Jacob Aborn sat up on the bench at the opposite side of the room. He said nothing as he watched her work, and his very silence told Nancy that he had given up all hope of escape. Presently, however, his interest quickened.

"You're getting it?" he demanded eagerly.

"I think so," Nancy returned.

Grimly she struggled to free herself. Her hands and wrists were now bleeding, but she was oblivious of the cuts and bruises. The realization that Stumpy Dowd was speeding toward River Heights to make trouble for Laura drove her to more frantic efforts. She must escape!

Then, without warning, the light in the lantern went out and the room was plunged in darkness. The supply of oil had been exhausted.

Nancy found it more difficult to work, but she kept doggedly on. Each minute seemed an eternity. Then after a quarter of an hour, success was hers.

With a cry of pleasure, she pulled her hands free from the ropes.

"I did it!" she cried.

Jacob Aborn sprang up from the bench, his chain clanking loudly against the floor.

"Then we'll escape! We may be able to catch that scoundrel yet!"

Nancy did not respond, for she was working grimly at the ropes which bound her feet. Stumpy had tied the knots securely and they were stubborn. She could have severed the ropes in an instant with a knife, but was forced to pick them out with her fingers. It was tedious work.

"There!" she exclaimed, as she untied the last knot. "I'm free!"

She sprang to her feet, and tottered uncertainly. The blow on her head had left her dizzy, and her limbs were cramped from lack of circulation. Leaning weakly against the wall, she recovered her equilibrium.

"Have courage!" she called out to Jacob Aborn. "I'll set you free in a minute if I can find the key!"

"It's hanging from a nail on the north wall," Mr. Aborn directed her eagerly.

Stumbling across the cellar, Nancy groped about on the damp wall. Stumpy had hung the key in plain sight of his two victims as a means of torturing them, but now his action served them to advantage.

Nancy struck a nail with her hand and the key clattered down at her feet. Fumbling about in the dark, she found it and ran to Jacob Aborn's side.

Quickly working at the padlock, she set the man free. The chains fell to the floor with a loud thud.

"Now to catch Stumpy Dowd!" she cried. "We must hurry or he will get away!"

"He had to go back to the house after the money," Jacob Aborn said tensely. "We may catch him there!"

CHAPTER XIX

In Pursuit

NANCY DREW urged Jacob Aborn to make haste, for she little realized to what desperate physical straits his long imprisonment had brought him. At the exultation of being free of his bonds, he had leaped to his feet in the dark cellar, eager to rush to the bungalow on the lake before Stumpy Dowd should have a chance to escape. But as he moved forward several steps, he felt his knees sink uncertainly.

Nancy, unaware of the physical anguish Jacob Aborn was enduring, groped about in the darkness for the bottom step of the stairway leading from the cellar. Presently her foot touched it, and she called out to her companion. He dragged himself to her side, scarcely able to walk.

"Are you ill, Mr. Aborn?" Nancy demanded anxiously. She could not see his face.

"Oh, no!" the man protested quickly. "I'm only a bit weak from being tied up like a dog in a kennel. My legs will be all right after I've used them a few minutes."

But try as he would, the man was unable to climb the stairway unassisted. Nancy, realizing his predicament, reached out a strong arm to help him.

Even then Jacob Aborn was forced to stop frequently for a brief rest, leaning upon Nancy for support while he recuperated his strength. But at last the top of the stairway was reached, and he then insisted that he was able to walk without her help.

Nancy led the way to the living room window, and after climbing out to the porch, assisted Jacob Aborn to crawl through the opening.

"What a relief!" he gasped, filling his lungs with pure air. "This is the first decent breath I've had in nearly two weeks!"

In the east, the moon was just rising over the forest, and stars were commencing to peep through the clouds which were now breaking up and drifting swiftly along the sky like scudding ships at sea. The cellar had accustomed Nancy's eyes to a blacker darkness than that which now faced her, and it was possible to make out objects well enough to pick the route through the forest. Yet, glancing uneasily at Jacob Aborn, she wondered if he would be able to walk the short distance to the roadster.

"Do you think you can make it?" she questioned. "It isn't far to my car."

"I think so," Laura's guardian declared grimly.

Nancy offered her arm again, and at a slow pace they walked across the clearing. Entering the forest, they had gone but a short way when Mr. Aborn sank down on a log along the trail, breathing heavily.

"I've got to rest," he murmured, his voice shaky from fatigue. "You go on without me, Nancy!"

"Just rest here for a moment, Mr. Aborn," Nancy said encouragingly. "I'm sure you will be all right in a few moments."

She was unwilling to desert Jacob Aborn, for if she went on ahead, she was afraid he would never reach the bungalow on the lake. At the same time, she was impatient at the delay. Already, Stumpy Dowd had a good half-hour's start. Unless they hurried, he would escape with Laura's fortune. Once he had left the bungalow it would be difficult to pick up his trail again.

"It's only a little way farther to the car," Nancy urged gently after Mr. Aborn had rested for a few minutes.

With an effort, he arose from the log and wavered unsteadily on his feet.

"I can make it now," he insisted. "We can't let that scoundrel escape!"

Leaning heavily on Nancy, he moved forward again, more rapidly than before. His breathing came hard, but he offered no complaint and refused to pause again even for a brief rest. His nerve carried him along. For Laura's sake he exerted himself to the utmost.

It was a walk that Nancy never forgot. Time and again Jacob Aborn stumbled and would have fallen headlong had it not been for the sturdy support the girl gave him.

"You'd better leave me and go ahead alone," he said several times. "I'm willing to try my best, but I know I can't make it."

"Oh, yes you can, Mr. Aborn," Nancy urged. "It's only a short distance now to the place where I left my roadster. As soon as we reach that you'll be safe."

"You're a very kind girl to do all this for me," murmured the exhausted man.

"We've got to do it. Think of Laura," and thus Nancy urged him forward.

Through the bushes and around a number of the rocks they stumbled. Once both went headlong, and Nancy had almost all the wind knocked out of her. But she picked herself up and managed to drag the man once more to his feet.

"How much farther?" he whispered hoarsely.

"Only a short distance," she answered as lightly as she could. "Keep up your courage and we're bound to get there."

Presently, with a feeling of relief, Nancy caught sight of her automobile standing in the bushes where she had left it. Although she had not mentioned her fears to Jacob Aborn, she had been afraid that Stumpy Dowd might have taken the car.

Hastily helping Laura's guardian into the the roadster, she sprang in after him and took her place behind the steering wheel. With nervous haste, she started the motor and backed around in the road. The car shot forward in a burst of speed.

Neither driver nor passenger exchanged a word as they raced madly toward the bungalow. Nancy had her hands full managing the steering wheel, for she was taking the rough road at dangerous speed.

Driving as near the bungalow as possible, she helped Mr. Aborn to alight.

Abandoning the automobile, they started afoot through the forest. As before, Nancy offered Mr. Aborn her arm, helping him along. She was relieved that he walked with less difficulty.

A few minutes, and they came to the clearing.

Directly ahead, they caught a glimpse of the house. To their disappointment the windows were dark.

"I'm afraid the bird has flown," Nancy observed quietly.

"It looks that way," Jacob Aborn admitted gloomily.

"Still, he may be there yet. The windows were dark earlier in the evening, and he was here then."

"At least, it will be wise to approach cautiously."

"Yes, we're unarmed and would be no match for him if he heard us coming. We don't want to place ourselves in his power a second time."

"Oh, if I can get my hands on that scoundrel!" Jacob Aborn gritted.

The thought gave him new strength, and he moved eagerly forward again. Cautiously, the two crept toward the house, approaching from the rear.

"You haven't a key, I suppose?" Nancy whispered.

"No. That villain took it away from me along with everything else."

"Never mind, I know a way to get in."

However, as Nancy drew near the bungalow, she saw that there was no need of a latchkey. The back door stood ajar, as though someone had fled without taking time to shut it.

With Mr. Aborn close behind her, Nancy Drew stepped cautiously into the kitchen. There was profound silence. The bungalow appeared deserted.

Crossing the room on tiptoe, she groped about on the kitchen table and found an oil lamp. Lighting it, she picked it up and hurried toward the living room.

Pausing in the doorway, she cast a critical glance about and saw that everything was in disorder. A chair had been overturned, a small rug was out of place, papers were scattered all about. The two suitcases which Stumpy Dowd had packed earlier in the evening were missing.

"He's escaped!" Nancy exclaimed in bitter disappointment as she surveyed the confusion.

Just then her eye fell upon the safe and she saw that the door was wide open. With a little cry of alarm she rushed across the room and looked inside. With the exception of a few papers, everything had been taken.

Snatching up the papers, Nancy hastily examined them. As she had feared, they were worthless.

"Laura's fortune!" she cried angrily. "That rascal has escaped with every penny of it!"

"Oh, my poor Laura!" Jacob Aborn groaned.

He moved heavily over to the safe and gave it one hopeless glance.

"He's taken everything of mine, too! I don't mind for myself—it's only that Laura must suffer for my negligence."

"It wasn't your fault, Mr. Aborn. We'll capture that man somehow! We must notify the police! I'll telephone the station this minute!"

"You can't. There isn't a phone in the house."

"You have no phone?" Nancy echoed. "Oh, what an aggravation!"

"Oh, why didn't I have one installed?" Jacob Aborn demanded of himself. "I always intended to."

"Where is the nearest one?"

"At the hotel."

"Then we must go there at once."

"I'm afraid it will be too late. That scoundrel has too great a start."

"We must try to capture him, anyway! With luck we can do it!"

"Yes, we must try!" Jacob Aborn exclaimed.

He started toward the door, but was forced to grasp the back of a chair for support. Nancy ran to him and eased him into the chair.

"You're too ill to go!" she cried.

One quick glance had assured her that he was on the verge of collapse. Only the hope that he might save Laura Pendleton's fortune had given him the strength to reach the bungalow. Now he was too nearly exhausted to go farther.

Mr. Aborn dropped his head on his hands.

"I guess I'm done up," he admitted.

"Of course you must stay here," Nancy insisted. "I'll send a doctor to you."

"Don't think about me. Just set the police on the trail of Stumpy Dowd!"

"I'll do both. And as soon as I telephone to the police, I intend to start after Stumpy myself."

"But the danger! You must think of your own safety!"

"I'll be careful," Nancy promised as she turned away. "Just stay here and rest until the doctor comes. I must hurry now. Every minute counts."

CHAPTER XX

NANCY'S DARING ACTION

LEAVING Jacob Aborn behind, Nancy Drew turned and ran from the bungalow. As she sped swiftly down the path, she passed the garage and halted long enough to glance inside.

Stumpy's racing car was gone. Nancy stooped down and examined the driveway, but it was too dark for her to see the wheel tracks. However, she was fairly certain that the man had taken the lake route, for there was no road through the forest in the immediate vicinity of the bungalow. Nancy had been forced to leave her own roadster a short distance away.

"It's not going to be easy to capture Stumpy," she thought. "A good many roads branch off from the lake thoroughfare. That man is a clever criminal and he'll take care to cover up his trail."

Running through the forest, she reached her roadster and sprang in. Quickly starting the motor, she headed the automobile down the road. To reach the Beach Cliff Hotel, it would be necessary for her to follow the forest a short distance until it joined the lake road. From there she would have a fairly straight, smooth stretch to the hotel.

The rough forest road held Nancy to a slow pace, but when she reached the lake thoroughfare she stepped on the accelerator, and the little car began to purr like a contented cat.

She soon caught a glimpse of the lights of the hotel, and a few minutes later brought the roadster to a halt in front of the inn. Without bothering to park the car according to the regulations, she sprang to the ground and ran inside.

As she entered the lobby, a number of persons turned and stared at her curiously. Nancy Drew was well aware that her hair was in disorder and that her clothing was in disarray, but she was indifferent to her appearance.

Rushing to a row of telephone booths, she saw at a glance that they were all in use. Without a moment's hesitation she rushed back to the main desk and, to the astonishment of the clerk in charge, snatched up his private telephone.

"The public telephones are at the end of the hall," he told her with pointed politeness.

"Sorry," Nancy apologized briefly. "This is a rush call."

Placing an emergency call for the police station, she waited impatiently. The hotel clerk, who had heard her directions to the telephone operator, underwent a sudden change of expression.

"Hello? Hello?" Nancy said frantically into the transmitter. "Police station?"

After a seemingly interminable wait, she was connected with the chief, and in a few terse sentences told what had happened.

"I think he must have taken the lake road," she finished. "He may be heading for River Heights before he strikes out for some distant point."

"We'll have a squad right after him," came the reassuring response.

Nancy hung up the receiver, and stood lost in thought for a moment.

"I must telephone to River Heights and warn Laura," she decided.

Again she placed a call, and waited impatiently for it to be put through. Several minutes passed and then at last the bell jangled. Eagerly she caught up the receiver and held it to her ear.

"Your party does not answer," came the precise voice of the operator.

"That's strange," Nancy thought, in alarm. "I can't understand why Laura didn't answer. Surely, she must be there, unless——"

Even in her mind, she dreaded to finish the sentence. Stumpy Dowd had threatened to go to River Heights and force Laura to hand over the jewels to him, but Nancy doubted that he could have reached the place so quickly. Still, it was only twenty miles away, and Stumpy's car was built for speed.

The thought that even now Laura might be in grave danger struck terror to Nancy Drew's heart. She would never forgive herself if anything happened to the girl while she was a guest in the Drew residence.

"If only father were at home, he could help me," she thought miserably.

The hotel clerk had overheard Nancy's conversation, and now regarded her with respect and curiosity.

"Is there anything I can do to help?" he inquired.

"Yes, send a doctor to Jacob Aborn's bungalow as quickly as you can."

"At once."

"And telephone to points along the road between here and River Heights, warning the police to be on the watch for a man in a racing car."

"How about the radio stations?"

"By all means! I can give you a description of the man."

Hastily, Nancy described Stumpy as best she

could. Before she had finished, a number of hotel guests had crowded about the desk, suspecting that something unusual had happened. They would have plied Nancy with questions which would have delayed her, had she not run from the lobby and jumped into her roadster.

A moment she hesitated uncertainly.

"The police may catch Stumpy, and again they may not," she told herself grimly. "I'm going to try to pick up the trail myself."

With sudden decision, she headed the car down the lake road. Although not paved, the highway was well dragged, and with a smooth stretch before her, Nancy Drew pressed her foot hard upon the gasoline pedal. The little blue car fairly roared down the road as though it, too, were eager to overtake Stumpy Dowd. Ordinarily, Nancy was not a fast driver, but now she knew that much depended upon her speed. Once Stumpy crossed the state line, it would be more difficult to cause his arrest.

Nancy Drew was a brave girl, and was too intent upon preventing the man's escape to consider seriously the danger which she might be running into herself. Alone and unarmed, she would find herself at a hopeless disadvantage should she meet the criminal face to face.

Presently, on a distant hill, Nancy caught the gleam of a headlight. Another automobile was coming toward her.

"I'll stop those people and ask if they've passed a racing car," she decided upon sudden impulse.

Bringing her automobile to an abrupt halt in the middle of the road, she signaled for the approaching car to stop. It was a brown sedan, and as it came within the range of her headlights, Nancy thought there was something familiar about it.

The automobile came to a stop not far from her roadster.

"Hello, there," a voice called out. "What's the matter?"

With a start, Nancy Drew recognized the voice.

CHAPTER XXI

Laura Begins to Worry

Not without misgiving, Laura Pendleton stood at the window of the Carson Drew residence and watched Nancy start off for Melrose Lake in her roadster.

"Perhaps I shouldn't have allowed her to take that note to my guardian," she thought uneasily. "Nancy is going to a great deal of trouble and risk for me. I'm afraid it isn't fair to involve her in my affairs."

After a time, she entered the library and tried to interest herself in a novel. She found she could not remember a word she had read, so laid the book aside in a little while. Walking restlessly to the window, she glanced out.

"I may as well do some shopping," she decided. "It will help me kill the time and help me forget my troubles."

She told Hannah Gruen where she was going, and then started off afoot for the business section of River Heights. The day was a pleasant one, and as she walked briskly along, her worries seemed less real.

Reaching a department store, Laura entered and purchased a few articles for which she had urgent need. In her hasty departure from Melrose Lake, she had forgotten a great many things. However, she made her purchases with the utmost caution, for with the exception of a twenty dollar bill in her purse, she was without funds. When that was gone she did not know what she would do.

"I'll never sell or pawn mother's jewels, even if I starve," she told herself. "I'll manage some way. Perhaps Nancy will help me find work."

Carrying her packages with her, Laura walked slowly back to the Drew residence. Already, the evening shadows were beginning to gather. In another hour or two it would be dark. As she passed the garage, she noticed that it was empty. Nancy had not returned.

"I do hope she gets back before dark," Laura thought anxiously.

Entering the house, she had not had time to put away her things when the telephone jangled. A minute later, the housekeeper told her that there was a long-distance telephone call for her.

"It's from Miss Nancy, I think," Hannah Gruen said.

"Oh, I hope nothing has happened!"

Eagerly, Laura snatched up the telephone

receiver. Nancy's quiet voice at the other end of the wire reassured her. However, as she listened to her friend's daring plan, she was somewhat alarmed. Still, other than to warn Nancy to be careful, she made no protest, for she felt that her friend's judgment was probably better than her own.

"If I'm not back or haven't telephoned within twenty-four hours, send the police to your guardian's bungalow," Nancy told her.

Laura promised, and a moment later hung up. Before she turned away from the telephone, she regretted that she had not asked Nancy to give up her plan.

"She doesn't realize what a mean man Jacob Aborn is," she told herself. "If he catches her prowling about the bungalow at night there's no telling what he may do."

Tempted to call Nancy back, she picked up the telephone again. With her hand on the receiver, she hesitated.

"I'm just a little coward," she accused herself. "I'll not let my nerves get the best of me this time."

Resolutely she turned away. Presently, Hannah called her to dinner, and she made a pretense of eating, but was relieved when the dessert dishes were cleared away. Returning to the living room, she tried to read the evening paper. The hours dragged slowly along, and still there was no sign of Nancy. Several times Laura walked to the window and cast a hopeful glance down the driveway.

"I suppose it's too early to expect her home," she told herself.

As she crossed to the window for perhaps the tenth time that evening she was surprised to see a tall, elderly man coming up the walk toward the house. Although Laura had never seen him before, she was instantly convinced that it was Carson Drew.

He thrust open the front door and his eyes fell upon her.

"Hello, Nancy," he called. "It's good to get back home again! Oh, I beg your pardon! I couldn't see your face. I thought you were my daughter."

"I don't wonder you are surprised to find a stranger in your home," Laura said, with a friendly smile.

Quickly, she introduced herself and told Carson Drew what had happened and why Nancy had gone to Melrose Lake. She ended by apologizing for her presence in the house.

"You're entirely welcome to our hospitality," Mr. Drew assured her cordially when she had finished her story. "But I'll admit I'm rather worried about Nancy. Tell me more about that guardian of yours. What does he look like?"

Laura gave a detailed description of the man.

"H-m! Did you say that his name is Jacob Aborn? Wait a minute."

Walking over to the desk he began to rummage in a drawer. Laura noticed the stern expression on his face and was troubled.

After a brief search, Carson Drew brought out a small photograph and handed it to Laura.

"Is that your guardian?"

Laura stared at the photograph in amazement.

"Why, it is! It's Jacob Aborn!"

Carson Drew shook his head.

"That man is Stumpy Dowd."

"I don't understand."

"Stumpy Dowd is a clever criminal. He has a long police record. Just now he is at large."

"Stumpy Dowd!" Laura exclaimed in horror. "You mean my guardian is a criminal?"

"It looks that way, and a particularly tough one at that."

"And Nancy has gone up there to see him! What if something should happen to her!"

"We must get in touch with her at once! Do you know the hotel where she is staying?"

"Yes. But it's pretty late now. Perhaps she isn't there."

"That's what we want to find out."

Now thoroughly excited, Laura ran to the telephone and placed a call to the Beach Cliff

Hotel. Impatiently, Carson Drew waited for a response. When the bell finally rang, he snatched up the receiver.

"Hello?" he said eagerly.

It was the voice of the hotel telephone operator that greeted him.

"We are unable to reach your party. Miss Drew is not in her room."

Carson Drew turned from the telephone, a drawn expression upon his face.

"She's not in," he informed Laura. "That may mean anything, and again it may not. I'm afraid Nancy is in trouble!"

"Oh, what shall we do?"

"I must go to Melrose Lake as quickly as I can."

"May I go too? It was my fault that Nancy went there, and I want to help if I can."

"We may run into danger."

"I'm not afraid."

Laura, who by nature was timid, had suddenly become calm and determined.

"Then get your things quickly."

As Carson Drew issued the order, he jerked open a drawer in the table and pulled out a revolver. Hastily loading it, he stuck it in his pocket.

"I'm ready," Laura announced.

Rushing from the house, they climbed into Mr. Drew's brown sedan. He backed out of the garage and without stopping to close the doors behind him, headed toward Melrose Lake.

"Oh, I hope we get there in time!" Laura breathed.

Carson Drew made no response, but his hands clenched more tightly on the steering wheel.

CHAPTER XXII

A Chance Meeting

Nancy Drew could scarcely believe her ears when she heard an answering shout from the automobile which had halted near her roadster. She recognized the voice of her father.

With a cry of joy, she sprang from the car and ran across the road toward the sedan.

"Father!" she cried.

"Nancy!"

As Carson Drew recognized his daughter, he hastily climbed out of the sedan and welcomed her into his arms.

"What a relief to find you safe and sound!" he exclaimed. "When Laura told me why you had gone to Melrose Lake, I was afraid for you. What has happened?"

"Oh, everything! I guess I'm lucky to be alive! But there's no time to tell you now. We must capture Stumpy Dowd first. He's escaping with Laura's fortune. Tell me, did you meet a racing car between here and River Heights?"

"Not that I recall."

"We met only two automobiles," Laura added, "and both were family cars."

"Then Stumpy didn't head for River Heights after all."

"He's probably striking for the state line," Carson Drew declared.

"The police will look for him on the River Heights road. Stumpy will escape unless we can pick up his trail ourselves. I was almost positive he took this road."

"Perhaps he turned off before he had gone very far," Carson Drew suggested. "We passed a branch road down here about five miles. He may have taken that."

"Where does it lead?"

"To Hamilton, and from there across the state line."

"Then he probably took that road. Oh, if we can catch him! He has such a head start!"

"Come on! We can do it!" Carson Drew cried. He turned quickly to Laura.

"Get in the roadster with Nancy," he ordered. "If it comes to a battle, you girls can drop back and be out of range of the bullets."

With alacrity, Laura obeyed. Nancy sprang in beside her. The motor of the roadster was already running, and she had only to shift gears to be off. She must pull out of the way before her father could turn his sedan in the road.

"I'll go on ahead," she shouted.

"All right. But if you see Stumpy's car, slow down and let me take the lead."

Shifting gears, Nancy was off at top speed. A few minutes later, Laura looked back and reported that Carson Drew was rapidly making up the distance he had lost.

Her eyes focused upon the road, Nancy Drew clung grimly to the wheel. The little figured ribbon in the speedometer crept higher and higher until the car wavered in the road. Reducing the speed slightly, she held her foot steady on the gasoline pedal.

A sharp curve would have been Nancy's undoing, but she was fairly familiar with the road and knew that for several miles she had a straight stretch before her.

"If only there isn't another wretched detour to be made!" the girl exclaimed.

But there was no detour and for that straight stretch Nancy did some of her fastest traveling, a rate of speed that often made Laura gasp in alarm.

"Oh, dear! don't jump the fence or climb a tree," gasped the girl.

"I won't," answered Nancy. "But hold tight."

Yet, even at the rapid rate she was traveling, she doubted that it would be possible to overtake Stumpy Dowd. She figured that he must have from fifteen to thirty minutes start, and his automobile was equipped with a special racing motor. Nancy's roadster was high-powered, but it was not reasonable to suppose that she could overtake the man unless luck favored her.

Removing her eyes from the road for one brief instant, Nancy glanced anxiously at the gasoline gauge on the dash. To her relief, the tank registered nearly three-quarters full. There was no need to worry on that score.

"Look!" Laura cried sharply.

Nancy's eyes came back to the road. Straight ahead she saw a small red light.

"It must be the tail light of an auto," Laura declared uneasily. "Can it be Stumpy?"

Nancy did not reply at once, for she was too intent upon watching. Although she promptly reduced the speed of her engine, she noticed that the light was gradually becoming larger. At first she thought she must be gaining on a car ahead. Then she decided that the light was not moving.

"I don't believe it can be Stumpy," she told Laura, "but we'll take no chances."

As the roadster slowed down, Carson Drew came closer in his sedan. Nancy was about to permit him to pass when she looked again at the red light. She was now close enough to see that it was a lantern. Speeding up, she came to an obstruction across the road and was forced to halt. Carson Drew pulled up alongside.

"We can take the road to the right," he shouted. "It leads to Hamilton. Stumpy must have taken it."

Nancy was staring at a sign which read:

Road under construction.
Travel at your own risk.

"How about this road straight ahead?" she demanded of her father.

"It's a short cut to Hamilton."

"Then why not take it?"

"It's closed for construction work."

"But it's not impassable, is it?"

"Probably not. But at night——"

"It's our only chance, father. We're so far behind Stumpy we'll never catch him unless we risk this short cut."

"You're right," Carson Drew said, with quick decision. "We'll try it, but we must drive carefully."

Springing from the sedan, he moved the barrier from the road and Nancy drove through. At first the highway seemed no different from the one she had been following, but before she had gone a mile, she saw the danger signs which were in the form of steam shovels, wagons, and machinery parked along the roadside.

"Be careful!" Laura warned her.

Soon the little roadster was wallowing in soft dirt, and each instant Nancy half expected the wheels to sink to the hubs. The engine pulled hard but did not stall. Nancy handled the wheel dexterously, weaving her way around objects in the road. Laura, who clung to the side of the car for dear life, was bounced roughly about.

At last, as the worst of it seemed to be over, Nancy relaxed slightly.

"Is father still coming?" she asked.

Laura looked back.

"Yes, he's right behind."

"Then I guess we're through safely. I can see a straight stretch ahead."

Again she stepped on the accelerator and the roadster responded with a burst of speed. In a few minutes she reached the end of the road. Laura hastily climbed out, and pulled away the barrier, permitting the two automobiles to enter the main road.

"We've cut off ten miles!" Nancy cried joyfully as Laura stepped back into the roadster. "If we're ever going to overtake Stumpy it ought to be in the next few minutes!"

As the little blue car plunged forward over the rough highway, the two girls kept gazing alertly into the darkness beyond the glare of the headlights, hoping to see the red tail light of Stumpy's automobile. As the minutes passed and still nothing appeared ahead, Nancy Drew began to grow alarmed.

After all, was it possible that she had made a mistake? Perhaps Stumpy had taken another road and even now was across the state line speeding toward the northern border. Laura expressed the fear.

"I'm afraid we're too late, Nancy."

"I'm not so sure about that, Laura!" Nancy's voice was electric.

"What do you see?" Laura demanded eagerly, as she saw her friend bending low over the wheel.

"A light! I think we're approaching a car!"

"I can't see anything."

"Just a minute. I think it went down behind that hill just ahead."

There was a long moment of suspense, and then Laura gave a little excited cry.

"Oh, now I see it!"

"And we're gaining," Nancy announced grimly. "I hope it's Stumpy!"

"Your father must have seen the light too," Laura informed Nancy, looking back. "He's coming closer. Hadn't we better let him go ahead?"

"Yes, I'll drop back in just a minute. But first I want to see if it is Stumpy."

Nancy could not increase the speed of the

roadster, for already she was going as rapidly as she dared. She was elated to observe that little by little she was creeping up on the car ahead.

Soon the headlights of her roadster played upon the back of the vehicle, and she observed that it was indeed a racing car. Even as she made the observation, the driver looked back. For an instant, his face was clearly illuminated. It was Stumpy Dowd!

CHAPTER XXIII

A Bad Turn

As Nancy Drew recognized Stumpy Dowd in the racing car directly ahead, she remembered her promise to her father and pulled to the side of the road. Carson Drew flashed by in the brown sedan. He, too, had recognized Stumpy.

Keeping close behind her father's automobile, Nancy kept her eyes on the red tail light. Stumpy, becoming aware that he was being followed, made a sudden burst of speed, and the distance between the cars was increasing.

"Oh, he's getting away," Laura cried anxiously.

"He'll not escape!" Nancy returned grimly. "Dad is speeding up, too!"

She, too, increased the speed of her roadster to keep in the race. And what a race it was! With utter disregard for safety, Stumpy's car lunged over the rough roads, closely followed by Carson Drew's sturdy sedan. To Nancy and Laura, who maintained the reckless pace, it seemed a miracle that the three automobiles remained between the fence posts.

"We're gaining again," Nancy observed a minute later.

Just then a shot rang out.

Carson Drew had fired as a warning for Stumpy to halt. Instead of stopping, he answered in kind.

There came a vivid flash of fire from his car, and an instant report. Stumpy had not shot into the air. A bullet whizzed dangerously close to the windshield of the brown sedan.

"Keep back, Nancy!" Carson Drew shouted.

The warning was lost in the roar of the wind. On and on the three cars raced. Stumpy gained ground, and then lost it again. Carson Drew approached nearer and nearer. He would soon be within gun range, and this time he intended to shoot at the automobile tires and force Stumpy to halt.

Nancy sensed that the end was drawing near, for it was apparent that the racing car had reached its maximum speed. Stumpy was making his last stand, and knew it. He looked back over his shoulder frequently now. Nancy had never seen such reckless driving. Where would the mad race end?

Suddenly, a look of horror came into Nancy's eyes. Straight ahead she saw a huge black and

white checkerboard sign at the side of the road.
Its significance sent a cold chill over her body.
There was a sharp curve to be made! At the
rate the three automobiles were traveling they
could never stay on the road!

Instantly, Nancy cut her throttle and
slammed on the brakes. But to her terror, she
saw that her father and Stumpy Dowd were
racing on. In their eagerness, they had failed
to see the warning sign.

Speeding up again for an instant, Nancy
leaned her head out the window and tried to
attract her father's attention.

"Stop!" she screamed frantically. "A
curve!"

Whether her father heard her or had seen
the danger himself she did not know, but he
slammed on his brakes. The sedan skidded
sideways, and for a moment Nancy held her
breath, fearful lest it turn turtle into the ditch.
By skillful manipulation of the steering wheel,
Carson Drew recovered control.

The moment she had warned her father,
Nancy tried to bring her own roadster to a
stop, but she had gained so much momentum
that she dared not slam on her brakes suddenly. Shutting off her gasoline and easing on
the foot brake gradually, she saw the curve
ahead and estimated that she would be able to

make it without overturning. Laura, her face pale and drawn, gripped the seat fearfully, but no cry escaped her.

It was Nancy who gave a frightened exclamation.

In the racing car ahead, Stumpy Dowd was oblivious of approaching danger. He looked back over his shoulder and waved tauntingly as he saw the distance between Nancy's car and his own rapidly increase.

"Look! Look! The curve!" Nancy shouted.

She had shouted the warning involuntarily, for a moment's reflection would have told her that Stumpy could not hear. Too late the man saw the danger.

He slammed on his emergency brake, but already the sharp curve was at hand.

The racing car turned turtle at the edge of the road, wavered an instant, then plunged over the side of a steep cliff!

"Oh!" Laura screamed. "He'll be killed!"

As Nancy rounded the curve in safety and brought the roadster to a quivering halt, she avoided for the moment looking down into the valley.

But for only an instant did she hesitate to view the wreck of the racing car. Springing from her roadster, she rushed to the edge of the road and courageously looked down over the cliff. Laura came running after her, and

Carson Drew, who had just brought his sedan alongside of the roadster, was close behind.

In horror, the three gazed down into the valley. The car had rolled nearly to the bottom of the little valley, and had overturned against a bowlder. A wheel had been torn loose from its axle and the body had been mashed in. There was no sign of Stumpy Dowd, but it was inconceivable that he could still be alive.

A silence held the trio as they gazed down upon the wreck and realized that their own fate might have been similar. At last Carson Drew found his voice.

"I guess it's all over with Stumpy now."

"Oh, he may be alive!" Nancy cried hopefully. "We must get him out of the wreckage!"

"You girls stay back," Mr. Drew said quietly, for he did not wish to expose them to a horrible sight. "I'll see what I can do."

"No, father, you'll need me to help if he's still alive. I'll go too," Nancy insisted.

Following her father, she lowered herself over the cliff and grasped the branch of a tiny tree to keep from falling. Laura hesitated a moment, and then, summoning all of her courage, scrambled after her friend.

The three rescuers half slid, half stumbled down the slope. There was no sound from the vicinity of the wreck.

"Stay back until I've had a look," Carson Drew warned the girls again.

Nancy intended to obey, for she had no desire to be the first to investigate the wreckage. But as she scrambled down the side of the cliff she saw a red flame flash up from the front end of the car.

She knew what that meant. The automobile had caught fire. With the gasoline tank in close proximity, there would soon be an explosion!

"Hurry! Hurry!" she urged her father.

Carson Drew had seen the flames, and he, too, realized the need for haste. Unless they worked quickly it would be impossible to get Stumpy's body from the wreck.

Sliding and falling down the slope, Nancy caught up with her father and together they rushed toward the automobile. Flames were leaping up from the front end. At any moment there might be an explosion.

The car was half overturned and rested against a large bowlder. Stumpy was pinned beneath the wreckage. With frantic haste, Nancy Drew and her father reached under the automobile and dragged the man out. He lay limp in their arms and it was with difficulty that they carried him away from the burning car.

"We got him out just in time," Mr. Drew

gasped as he carefully placed Stumpy on the ground.

Nancy looked back at the burning car and gave a little scream.

"The money! Laura's fortune!"

Before Carson Drew could restrain her, she ran back toward the wreck.

"Come back!" her father shouted.

Nancy did not pause. Throwing caution to the wind, she reached the wreck and groped about frantically. Her hand struck a suitcase and she dragged it out.

The heat was now almost unbearable, but Nancy would not be defeated. She knew there was another suitcase, and she was determined to save it.

Diving under the car for a second time, she found the bag and triumphantly brought it out, only to be jerked from the scene by her father.

"Nancy! Nancy!" he cried. "Are you mad! Those suitcases aren't worth your life!"

There was a sudden explosion. Instantly the combustible parts of the car ignited and the dry grass in the immediate vicinity began to burn.

As Nancy Drew realized what a narrow escape she had had, she trembled slightly.

"Oh, Nancy!" Laura clung weakly to her. "If anything had happened to you——"

"Well, I wanted to get those suitcases," she defended her action.

"What if they had burned?" Carson Drew demanded.

"Then Laura would have been without her fortune. All her money is in those two suitcases, unless I miss my guess."

"My money?" Laura gasped. "Then I do have a fortune?"

"You certainly have," Nancy assured her.

"And you risked your life to save it for me! Oh, how can I ever repay you?"

"Don't think about that now," Nancy said quickly. "I have a long story to tell you, but it must wait. Our first duty is to look after Stumpy."

Carson Drew had already turned his attention to the inert form which lay on the ground. A deep gash had been cut in Stumpy's forehead, and his right arm had been badly broken. His face was deathly white, and he did not appear to be breathing.

CHAPTER XXIV

STUMPY'S FATE

"I AM afraid—" began Carson Drew, but did not finish the sentence. Instead, he leaned over Stumpy Dowd and placed his fingers on the man's pulse.

"Is—is he dead?" Nancy asked fearfully, after a few moments.

Carson Drew relinquished Stumpy's wrist and turned grave eyes upon his daughter.

"He's still alive, but his heart action is very weak. I don't believe we'll be able to get him to the hospital."

"But we must try!"

"Yes, of course. But it's not going to be easy to get him to the automobile."

"There's a blanket in my roadster. Perhaps we could carry him on that."

"I believe we could."

"Then I'll get it."

Nancy scrambled up the cliff to the road and returned in a few minutes with the blanket. The unconscious Stumpy was lifted gently and placed upon it.

Mr. Drew and the two girls gathered up the corners and began the difficult climb. As they carried him to the automobile, Stumpy gave no sign of recovering consciousness.

"I'm afraid we can't do him much good," Mr. Drew commented, as they stretched him out on the rear seat of the sedan.

"I believe he's recovering consciousness," Nancy observed quietly.

As she spoke the man stirred slightly and groaned.

"That's an encouraging sign," Carson Drew declared. "We'll rush him to the hospital at Hamilton."

"I'll go back after the suitcases, and catch up with you later," Nancy suggested.

"All right. That will be wisest, I guess. We must rush Stumpy to the hospital without a minute's delay." He turned to Laura. "Perhaps you had better ride with me and keep an eye on Stumpy. I don't think he will recover enough to make trouble, but someone had best watch him. You don't mind?"

"Of course not."

Laura climbed into the sedan with the lawyer, and Nancy watched them drive away. Then she hurriedly descended the cliff and picked up the two suitcases. She was tempted to open them to make sure that Laura's fortune was inside, but upon second thought de-

cided that it would take too much time. She
must speed after her father and Laura.

Dragging the heavy suitcases up the slope,
she deposited them in the roadster, and started
down the road after the sedan. Although she
drove rapidly, she did not overtake her father.
Reaching Hamilton, she stopped at a gasoline
station and asked the way to the police hospital.

Arriving there, she saw her father's sedan
parked outside. Leaving the two precious
suitcases inside the roadster, she locked both
doors and ran inside. Laura was standing
near the door and Carson Drew was talking
with the authorities. Presently, he came over
to Nancy and Laura, bringing a distinguished-
looking man with him.

Quietly he presented Mr. Howland, the chief
of police. The man bowed to both girls, but his
eyes lingered upon Nancy after the introduction had been completed.

"I have just learned of the part you played
in the daring capture of Stumpy Dowd," he
said to her. "Allow me to congratulate you."

The chief of police extended his hand, and
Nancy Drew accepted it with a pleased smile.

"It was really nothing," she protested mod-
estly. "I would never have been suspicious of
the man if I hadn't been trying to help my
friend. Even after I discovered his identity,
I might have fallen down on the job if father

hadn't come along at the critical moment."

"I'm not sure about that, Miss Drew," and the chief smiled. "You strike me as a very resourceful young lady."

"Suppose there is no question that the man is really Stumpy Dowd?" Nancy inquired. She was eager to change the subject to a less personal one.

"Not the slightest. I came to the hospital just as soon as I was notified that he had been captured and identified him myself. I would know that face anywhere. He's been in the rogues' gallery for a good many years, but has managed to keep out of the way of the police. He's led us a merry chase!"

"Will he live?"

"Stumpy is on the operating table now," Carson Drew explained to Nancy. "The doctor considers his condition very grave, but he may pull through."

"And if he does he'll get a long term in prison," the chief added.

Nancy was pressed for details of her part in the capture of the man. However, in telling her story, she did not mention Jacob Aborn, for she wished to surprise Laura later.

"We may as well go back home," Carson Drew said presently. "It may be hours before we learn anything definite about Stumpy's condition."

"If you'll give me your telephone number, I'll see to it that you are kept informed," the chief promised.

After Mr. Drew had written his address and telephone number on a slip of paper, the three left the building.

"Ho-hum!" Carson Drew yawned sleepily. "I think it's time we were all in bed."

"Not yet," Nancy declared importantly. "We must return to Melrose Lake."

"Why should we go back there?"

"I'll tell you when we get there," Nancy announced mysteriously. "It's a surprise."

"Well, just as you say," her father grumbled good-naturedly. "But I hope the surprise is worth while, because I'm tired."

With Laura and Nancy riding in the roadster, the two automobiles started off for Melrose Lake. This time, however, they traveled at a moderate rate of speed.

"Where in the world are we going?" Laura questioned, as Nancy turned into a familiar side road. "Aren't we heading toward my guardian's bungalow?"

It was with difficulty that she spoke the word "guardian."

"Yes," Nancy admitted.

"Oh, why are we going back there? After all that has happened I don't believe I shall ever want to go back!"

Nancy reached out and patted Laura's hand reassuringly.

"Just trust me," she said smilingly.

Nancy had selected the lake route and was able to drive the roadster very nearly to the doorstep of the Aborn bungalow. Stopping the car, she waited for her father, who was a short way behind.

"Why, there's a light inside the house!" Laura exclaimed. "And I can see someone moving about!"

Nancy Drew smiled and began to unload the suitcases from the back of the roadster.

"What are you up to, anyway?" Mr. Drew demanded, as he stepped out of his sedan and came toward the girls.

"You'll soon find out," Nancy laughed.

"Here, I'll carry those suitcases," Mr. Drew picked up the two bags and followed Nancy down the path toward the bungalow.

Laura held back rather reluctantly, but Nancy kept pulling her along. Boldly she opened the front door and stepped into the lighted living room.

"Laura!" a low voice murmured.

Jacob Aborn arose from a chair and held out his arms.

Laura hesitated, and glanced uncertainly from Nancy to Jacob Aborn.

"Your real guardian," Nancy said, "Jacob Aborn!"

"My guardian! Oh!"

With a little cry of joy, Laura went to him. For several minutes Nancy and her father stood quietly watching the happy homecoming. Then at last, they were swept into the conversation again.

"Did the doctor come?" Nancy inquired, for she observed that Mr. Aborn appeared much stronger than when she had left him a few hours before.

"Yes, thanks to your kindness, Miss Drew. He said he thought I would be all right in a few days. I feel much better already."

"I'm glad of that."

"I worried a great deal about you after you left. What happened? Did you catch that scoundrel?"

Nancy was forced to repeat the story a second time, and for the benefit of her father and Laura, added the details of her imprisonment in the deserted bungalow.

"You took a great deal of risk," Mr. Drew chided his daughter. "But I must admit it was a clever piece of detective work."

"Thanks, dad."

" 'All's well that ends well,' " Mr. Aborn quoted rather tritely. "But in this case it didn't end well."

"What do you mean?" Nancy asked quickly.

"Laura has lost her fortune and I am penniless, too."

"Oh, no, Mr. Aborn! We recovered the money."

"I thought it burned up in the wreck."

"I should say not," Laura broke in. "Nancy dragged those suitcases out of the fire at the risk of her life."

"And to think we haven't even looked to see if the money is there!" Nancy exclaimed. "I guess we've been too busy the last hour."

"Let's have a look now," Mr. Drew proposed.

Picking up one of the suitcases, he examined it critically.

"Locked!" he announced. "And Stumpy probably has the key!"

"Oh, how disappointing," Laura murmured.

"If there's a hammer in the house, we can soon have these bags open!" the lawyer declared.

"I know where to find one!" Laura cried eagerly. "I'll get it."

In a few minutes she returned from the kitchen and gave the hammer to Mr. Drew. After a few sharp blows, the lock burst open.

Anxiously, the four looked inside. Carson Drew pulled out a great deal of clothing, but a careful examination revealed nothing of value.

"Oh, the money isn't there!" Nancy exclaimed in bitter disappointment. "What could have become of it?"

"There's another bag," her father reminded her.

The lock was stubborn, but several hard blows broke it. As Mr. Drew pushed back the cover there was a chorus of "ohs!" for there on top of a pile of clothing were the missing bank notes.

Jacob Aborn snatched up the neat packages of bills and hastily counted them. Mr. Drew continued his search through the suitcase and unearthed a small bundle of papers which he turned over to Laura's guardian.

"My property!" Jacob Aborn declared.

"Is Laura's money all here?" Nancy asked.

"Every cent of it."

"Then I'm really not poor, after all," Laura said happily. "Stumpy told me I was practically a pauper."

"A pauper! Why, you're rich. Your fortune amounts to more than a hundred thousand dollars!"

"A hundred thousand dollars! Oh, I can scarcely believe it."

"You deserve every cent of it," Nancy said kindly.

"The nicest part of all is that I have a guardian to love me," Laura returned wistfully.

"And a guardian who will always try to make you happy," Mr. Aborn added feelingly. "You have suffered a great deal the last few weeks. I will do my best to make it up to you."

"And I'll look after you, too. You'll need a good nurse for a few days."

"Then we'll leave you in good hands," Mr. Drew said as he picked up his hat. "I gather that you don't care to return to River Heights with us now."

"Oh, no!" Laura said quickly, and then bit her lip and flushed. "I didn't mean that the way it sounded. You don't know how I appreciate everything you've done for me; but it's just that I want to stay with my own guardian."

"We understand," Nancy said kindly, as she took Laura's hand in her own. "I'll send your things to-morrow."

"But I'll see you often, shan't I?"

"I hope so, Laura."

"River Heights is only twenty miles away. You must drive up often," Mr. Aborn put in.

Laura thought for a moment.

"Promise you'll come next Sunday," she begged. "You and your father must both come. I have a special reason for asking."

"Do," urged Mr. Aborn.

"All right, we'll come."

After Jacob Aborn and Laura had again

thanked Nancy and her father for what they
had done, the two said good-bye and left the
bungalow. As they stepped out on the porch,
Nancy chanced to turn her eyes toward the
east, and a startled expression came into her
face.

"What's the matter now?" Mr. Drew asked.

"The sun! It's just coming up over the lake!
We've been up all night."

"I feel like it, too," her father grumbled.

Nancy Drew did not hear, for she had turned
toward the east again and was observing the
glory of the sunrise. It was symbolic, she told
herself, not only of a new day, but of a new
life for Laura Pendleton.

CHAPTER XXV

LAURA'S GRATITUDE

NANCY DREW and her father did not forget their promise to call again at Jacob Aborn's bungalow, and the following Sunday afternoon found them on the way to Melrose Lake.

They started directly after a midday dinner which had been a rather silent meal.

It had rained a bit during the early morning but now the sun was shining brightly and there was just enough breeze to make it pleasant.

Nancy was driving her roadster while her father sat beside her, an unlighted cigar between his lips. Neither said a word until the town was left far behind and they were drawing towards the country of the lakes.

"What are you thinking of, Nancy?" questioned her father at last.

"I was thinking of Laura and of Mr. Aborn," she replied. "I was wondering if everything is turning out all right."

"It ought to—with Stumpy out of the way," answered Carson Drew.

"So it would seem. But Laura is such an unusual girl—and she went through so much. I'd hate to see her break down and have a spell of sickness."

"Oh, joy seldom hurts anyone, Nancy. Its real sorrow that pulls a person down."

"I certainly hope the real Mr. Aborn proves to be all right."

"I think I'm a pretty good judge of character, and he looked all right to me."

A little later they passed the spot where Nancy had first met Laura during the awful storm—when the terror-stricken girl was on her way to the Drew homestead. How many things had happened since then!

Then they came in sight of the bungalow.

As they drove up in the blue roadster, Laura Pendleton ran from the house and greeted them enthusiastically. She was dressed in a bright blue frock and seemed happier than Nancy had ever seen her. The change was remarkable. Her eyes were bright and her cheeks were beginning to fill out a trifle.

"Oh, I'm so glad you came!" Laura cried eagerly, as she led them toward the bungalow.

As the two girls walked up the path arm in arm, Nancy lowered her voice.

"How do you like your guardian?" she asked.

"Oh, Nancy, he's the kindest man in the world. He's so good to me."

"I'm glad that you are happy here, Laura," and Nancy smiled. "You didn't like the bungalow at first, you know."

"Oh, it wasn't the house! It was Stumpy Dowd! Everything has changed now. My guardian is planning so many wonderful things for me! But I'll tell you about that later."

"How is Mr. Aborn?" Nancy inquired solicitously.

They had reached the porch by this time, and Jacob Aborn himself opened the door. He had heard Nancy's question.

"I never felt better in my life," he assured her. "I've had a wonderful nurse."

Mr. Aborn drew up comfortable chairs for the two guests and sat down beside Laura on the davenport. After the four had chatted for some time, a maid served tea. Over the cups, Mr. Aborn told of his plans for his ward.

"I want her to rest this summer and enjoy her friends," he declared. "This fall, if I feel I can part with her for a few months, I'll send her to a girls' school. You'll like that, Laura?"

"Oh, I'll love it! I've always dreamed of going to a boarding school. But of course I shan't want to leave you."

"Don't worry on that score, Laura. I'll

probably spend most of my time coming to visit you.''

"You're spoiling me," Laura laughed. She turned to Nancy. "Mr. Aborn is planning so many wonderful things for me. He's building a tennis court in the yard, and I'm going to take swimming lessons!"

"I want to get Laura a motorboat," Mr. Aborn explained. "But think she should know how to swim first."

"And the nicest of all—I'm to have a new roadster something like yours, Nancy."

"Then you'll be able to drive over to River Heights and see me often."

"Indeed I will. And you and your friend, Helen Corning, must come here. We'll have regular week end parties!"

"By the way," Jacob Aborn turned to Mr. Drew, abruptly changing the subject. "Have you learned anything about Stumpy Dowd?"

"Why, yes, I thought you knew."

"I've heard nothing."

"The Hamilton chief of police telephoned yesterday. You'll not be bothered by that man again."

"You mean—he's dead?"

"Oh, no," Nancy broke in hastily. "His injuries weren't as serious as the doctor at first thought. He has been removed from the hospital and sent to jail. He'll probably get twenty-five years, eh, Dad?"

"Thirty, I believe," her father corrected.

Jacob Aborn nodded in satisfaction.

"Well, he'll receive his just due at that. When I think of the way that man tried to rob Laura——"

"Oh, Nancy, we owe you so much," Laura said earnestly. "You saved my guardian's life and you recovered my fortune."

"I hope you haven't forgotten the night on Moon Lake when you rescued Helen and me," Nancy reminded her, with a smile. "It isn't all one-sided, you see."

"But you've repaid the debt threefold."

"Laura and I have been talking it over," Mr. Aborn said quietly. "We have been trying to think of a way to thank you."

"Oh, I don't want any thanks," Nancy returned hastily. "I really enjoyed the adventure."

"I can't say that I did," Mr. Aborn responded ruefully. "Two weeks in a dungeon!"

"Nancy, you must accept some reward for what you did," Laura insisted, returning to the original subject.

Nancy shook her head stubbornly.

"But I have a fortune in my own name! Unless I give you money I don't know how to reward you."

"My reward is to know that you are happy, Laura."

"It's so kind of you to say that, but I don't feel right——"

"I don't want to hurt your feelings, Laura, but really I can't accept a reward."

"My daughter has solved a number of baffling mystery cases, and has made a point never to take pay for her work," Mr. Drew explained, coming to Nancy's rescue.

"It doesn't seem right not to give her anything."

"Nancy has accepted a number of souvenirs, as reminders of her various adventures."

"Oh, I remember now!" Laura cried eagerly. "Helen Corning told me."

"I did take an old mantel clock for solving the mystery of the missing Crowley will," Nancy admitted. "And I accepted a silver urn for discovering the ghost of the Turnbull mansion."

"Then it's only right that you accept a souvenir for solving the mystery of the deserted bungalow. Will you?"

"Well—" Nancy hesitated.

"Say, yes! It will make me feel so much better!"

"All right, I agree."

Laura sprang from the davenport and hurried upstairs to her room. In a few minutes she returned, bearing a tiny jewel case.

"It isn't half enough," she declared, handing Nancy the box.

"Oh, Laura, I'm afraid you've given me something expensive!"

She lifted the cover of the box and gazed at the contents. The jewel case contained a beautiful pendant of precious stones.

Nancy gave a little exclamation of surprise and delight as she held the necklace to the light.

"Oh, Laura!" she breathed. "It's gorgeous! But of course I can't keep it."

"Oh, you must! Why, you promised!"

"I said I would accept a souvenir, but I never dreamed you would give me anything so expensive. Didn't this pendant belong to your mother?"

"Yes. But that is no reason for you to refuse to take it. She would want me to give it to you."

"But it's such a precious keepsake to give away."

"It is precious," Laura admitted quietly. "But I have other pieces that mother left me. There is no one in the world I'd rather see have it than you. If it were not precious I would not offer it. Please take it, Nancy."

Laura's expression was so earnest and pleading that Nancy Drew could not find it in her heart to refuse. After all, she had given her promise.

"I will keep it," she said, with sudden decision. "And I'll always prize it highly."

After that, the conversation shifted to less personal subjects, and the afternoon passed quickly. Before Mr. Drew and his daughter departed, Laura escorted Nancy about the place, showing her the garden, the new boathouse, and the site for the tennis court.

"Only a week ago I fairly hated this place," she said thoughtfully. "And now I love it!"

"A great deal has happened since that stormy night on Moon Lake when we first met," Nancy returned musingly. "As I look back, it doesn't seem possible we could have packed so much adventure into one short month."

"No, it doesn't, but the adventures were mostly yours."

"I seem to have a way of getting into the thick of things," Nancy laughed. "Oh, well, everything came out right, and the nicest part of all is that you have found a happy home."

"And wonderful friends!"

An understanding silence fell upon the two girls, and for several moments they stood arm in arm, looking out across the lake. Presently, as they slowly moved on again, Laura Pendleton turned to her friend with a twinkle in her eyes.

"You've started quite a career for yourself, Nancy. I wonder if you'll have any more adventures?"

Nancy gave a tired sigh.

"Oh, I think I've had enough to last me for the rest of my life!" But in her heart, she knew she had not. The love for mystery would always be with her.

And Nancy Drew's adventuring days were by no means over. It was written in the annals of the future that before many months had elapsed she would be engrossed in a problem as puzzling as the bungalow mystery—a problem which would tax her mental powers and ingenuity to the limit.

But for the present, Nancy Drew was not pining for excitement or adventure. The prospect of a restful summer with Laura Pendleton and Helen Corning satisfied her completely.

THE END

This Isn't All!

Would you like to know what became of the good friends you have made in this book?

Would you like to read other stories continuing their adventures and experiences, or other books quite as entertaining by the same author?

On the *reverse side* of the wrapper which comes with this book, you will find a wonderful list of stories which you can buy at the same store where you got this book.

Don't throw away the Wrapper

Use it as a handy catalog of the books you want some day to have. But in case you do mislay it, write to the Publishers for a complete catalog.

THE TED SCOTT FLYING STORIES
By FRANKLIN W. DIXON

**Individual Colored Wrappers and Text Illustrations by
WALTER S. ROGERS
Each Volume Complete in Itself.**

No subject has so thoroughly caught the imagination of young America as aviation. This series has been inspired by recent daring feats of the air, and is dedicated to Lindberg, Byrd, Chamberlin and other heroes of the skies.

GROSSET & DUNLAP, *Publishers,* NEW YORK

THE FAMOUS ROVER BOYS SERIES

By ARTHUR M. WINFIELD

(EDWARD STRATEMEYER)

Beautiful Wrappers in Full Color

No stories for boys ever published have attained the tremendous popularity of this famous series. Since the publication of the first volume, The Rover Boys at School, some years ago, over three million copies of these books have been sold. They are well written stories dealing with the Rover boys in a great many different kinds of activities and adventures. Each volume holds something of interest to every adventure loving boy.

A complete list of titles is printed on the opposite page.

FAMOUS ROVER BOYS SERIES

BY ARTHUR M. WINFIELD
(Edward Stratemeyer)

OVER THREE MILLION COPIES SOLD OF THIS SERIES.

**Uniform Style of Binding.   Colored Wrappers.
Every Volume Complete in Itself.**

THE ROVER BOYS AT SCHOOL
THE ROVER BOYS ON THE OCEAN
THE ROVER BOYS IN THE JUNGLE
THE ROVER BOYS OUT WEST
THE ROVER BOYS ON THE GREAT LAKES
THE ROVER BOYS IN THE MOUNTAINS
THE ROVER BOYS ON LAND AND SEA
THE ROVER BOYS IN CAMP
THE ROVER BOYS ON THE RIVER
THE ROVER BOYS ON THE PLAINS
THE ROVER BOYS IN SOUTHERN WATERS
THE ROVER BOYS ON THE FARM
THE ROVER BOYS ON TREASURE ISLE
THE ROVER BOYS AT COLLEGE
THE ROVER BOYS DOWN EAST
THE ROVER BOYS IN THE AIR
THE ROVER BOYS IN NEW YORK
THE ROVER BOYS IN ALASKA
THE ROVER BOYS IN BUSINESS
THE ROVER BOYS ON A TOUR
THE ROVER BOYS AT COLBY HALL
THE ROVER BOYS ON SNOWSHOE ISLAND
THE ROVER BOYS UNDER CANVAS
THE ROVER BOYS ON A HUNT
THE ROVER BOYS IN THE LAND OF LUCK
THE ROVER BOYS AT BIG HORN RANCH
THE ROVER BOYS AT BIG BEAR LAKE
THE ROVER BOYS SHIPWRECKED
THE ROVER BOYS ON SUNSET TRAIL
THE ROVER BOYS WINNING A FORTUNE

GROSSET & DUNLAP,   PUBLISHERS,   NEW YORK

THE TOM SWIFT SERIES
By VICTOR APPLETON

Uniform Style of Binding. Individual Colored Wrappers.
Every Volume Complete in Itself.

Every boy possesses some form of inventive genius. Tom Swift is a bright, ingenious boy and his inventions and adventures make the most interesting kind of reading.

TOM SWIFT AND HIS MOTOR CYCLE
TOM SWIFT AND HIS MOTOR BOAT
TOM SWIFT AND HIS AIRSHIP
TOM SWIFT AND HIS SUBMARINE BOAT
TOM SWIFT AND HIS WIRELESS MESSAGE
TOM SWIFT AND HIS ELECTRIC RUNABOUT
TOM SWIFT AMONG THE DIAMOND MAKERS
TOM SWIFT IN THE CAVES OF ICE
TOM SWIFT AND HIS SKY RACER
TOM SWIFT AND HIS ELECTRIC RIFLE
TOM SWIFT IN THE CITY OF GOLD
TOM SWIFT AND HIS AIR GLIDER
TOM SWIFT IN CAPTIVITY
TOM SWIFT AND HIS WIZARD CAMERA
TOM SWIFT AND HIS GREAT SEARCHLIGHT
TOM SWIFT AND HIS GIANT CANNON
TOM SWIFT AND HIS PHOTO TELEPHONE
TOM SWIFT AND HIS AERIAL WARSHIP
TOM SWIFT AND HIS BIG TUNNEL
TOM SWIFT IN THE LAND OF WONDERS
TOM SWIFT AND HIS WAR TANK
TOM SWIFT AND HIS AIR SCOUT
TOM SWIFT AND HIS UNDERSEA SEARCH
TOM SWIFT AMONG THE FIRE FIGHTERS
TOM SWIFT AND HIS ELECTRIC LOCOMOTIVE
TOM SWIFT AND HIS FLYING BOAT
TOM SWIFT AND HIS GREAT OIL GUSHER
TOM SWIFT AND HIS CHEST OF SECRETS
TOM SWIFT AND HIS AIRLINE EXPRESS
TOM SWIFT CIRCLING THE GLOBE
TOM SWIFT AND HIS TALKING PICTURES
TOM SWIFT AND HIS HOUSE ON WHEELS
TOM SWIFT AND HIS BIG DIRIGIBLE

GROSSET & DUNLAP, *Publishers*, NEW YORK

THE DON STURDY SERIES
By VICTOR APPLETON

**Individual Colored Wrappers and Text Illustrations by
WALTER S. ROGERS
Every Volume Complete in Itself.**

In company with his uncles, one a mighty hunter and the other a noted scientist, Don Sturdy travels far and wide, gaining much useful knowledge and meeting many thrilling adventures.

DON STURDY ON THE DESERT OF MYSTERY;
An engrossing tale of the Sahara Desert, of encounters with wild animals and crafty Arabs.

DON STURDY WITH THE BIG SNAKE HUNTERS;
Don's uncle, the hunter, took an order for some of the biggest snakes to be found in South America—to be delivered alive !

DON STURDY IN THE TOMBS OF GOLD;
A fascinating tale of exploration and adventure in the Valley of Kings in Egypt.

DON STURDY ACROSS THE NORTH POLE;
A great polar blizzard nearly wrecks the airship of the explorers.

DON STURDY IN THE LAND OF VOLCANOES;
An absorbing tale of adventures among the volcanoes of Alaska.

DON STURDY IN THE PORT OF LOST SHIPS;
This story is just full of exciting and fearful experiences on the sea.

DON STURDY AMONG THE GORILLAS;
A thrilling story of adventure in darkest Africa. Don is carried over a mighty waterfall into the heart of gorilla land.

DON STURDY CAPTURED BY HEAD HUNTERS ;
Don and his party are wrecked in Borneo and have thrilling adventures among the head hunters.

DON STURDY IN LION LAND;
Don and his uncles organize an expedition to capture some extra large lions alive.

GROSSET & DUNLAP, *Publishers*, NEW YORK

THE RADIO BOYS SERIES

(Trademark Registered)

By ALLEN CHAPMAN

Author of the "Railroad Series," Etc.

**Individual Colored Wrappers. Illustrated.
Every Volume Complete in Itself.**

A new series for boys giving full details of radio work, both in sending and receiving—telling how small and large amateur sets can be made and operated, and how some boys got a lot of fun and adventure out of what they did. Each volume from first to last is so thoroughly fascinating, so strictly up-to-date and accurate, we feel sure all lads will peruse them with great delight.

Each volume has a Foreword by Jack Binns, the well-known radio expert.

THE RADIO BOYS' FIRST WIRELESS

THE RADIO BOYS AT OCEAN POINT

THE RADIO BOYS AT THE SENDING STATION

THE RADIO BOYS AT MOUNTAIN PASS

THE RADIO BOYS TRAILING A VOICE

THE RADIO BOYS WITH THE FOREST RANGERS

THE RADIO BOYS WITH THE ICEBERG PATROL

THE RADIO BOYS WITH THE FLOOD FIGHTERS

THE RADIO BOYS ON SIGNAL ISLAND

THE RADIO BOYS IN GOLD VALLEY

THE RADIO BOYS AIDING THE SNOWBOUND

THE RADIO BOYS ON THE PACIFIC

GROSSET & DUNLAP, *Publishers,* NEW YORK

THE BLYTHE GIRLS BOOKS

By LAURA LEE HOPE

Author of The Outdoor Girls Series

Illustrated by Thelma Gooch

The Blythe Girls, three in number, were left alone in New York City. Helen, who went in for art and music, kept the little flat uptown, while Margy, just out of business school, obtained a position as secretary and Rose, plain-spoken and business-like, took what she called a "job" in a department store. The experiences of these girls make fascinating reading—life in the great metropolis is thrilling and full of strange adventures and surprises.

GROSSET & DUNLAP *Publishers* NEW YORK

FOR HER MAJESTY—THE GIRL OF TODAY

THE POLLY BREWSTER BOOKS
By LILLIAN ELIZABETH ROY

Polly and Eleanor have many interesting adventures on their travels which take them to all corners of the globe.

POLLY OF PEBBLY PIT
POLLY AND ELEANOR
POLLY IN NEW YORK
POLLY AND HER FRIENDS
    ABROAD
POLLY'S BUSINESS VEN-
    TURE
POLLY'S SOUTHERN CRUISE

POLLY IN SOUTH
    AMERICA
POLLY IN THE SOUTH-
    WEST
POLLY IN ALASKA
POLLY IN THE ORIENT
POLLY IN EGYPT
POLLY'S NEW FRIEND

POLLY AND CAROLA

THE GIRL SCOUTS BOOKS
By LILLIAN ELIZABETH ROY

The fun of living in the woods, of learning woodcraft, of canoe trips, of venturing into the wilderness.

GIRL SCOUTS AT DANDELION CAMP
GIRL SCOUTS IN THE ADIRONDACKS
GIRL SCOUTS IN THE ROCKIES
GIRL SCOUTS IN ARIZONA AND NEW MEXICO
GIRL SCOUTS IN THE REDWOODS
GIRL SCOUTS IN THE MAGIC CITY
OIRL SCOUTS IN GLACIER PARK

THE WOODCRAFT GIRLS AT CAMP
THE WOODCRAFT GIRLS IN THE CITY
THE WOODCRAFT GIRLS CAMPING IN MAINE
THE LITTLE WOODCRAFTER'S BOOK
THE LITTLE WOODCRAFTER'S FUN ON THE FARM

GROSSET & DUNLAP,   PUBLISHERS,   NEW YORK

THE LILIAN GARIS BOOKS

Illustrated. Every volume complete in itself.

Among her "fan" letters Lilian Garis receives some flattering testimonials of her girl readers' interest in her stories. From a class of thirty comes a vote of twenty-five naming her as their favorite author. Perhaps it is the element of live mystery that Mrs. Garis always builds her stories upon, or perhaps it is because the girls easily can translate her own sincere interest in themselves from the stories. At any rate her books prosper through the changing conditions of these times, giving pleasure, satisfaction, and, incidentally, that tactful word of inspiration, so important in literature for young girls. Mrs. Garis prefers to call her books "juvenile novels" and in them romance is never lacking.

GROSSET & DUNLAP *Publishers* NEW YORK

THE OUTDOOR GIRLS SERIES
by LAURA LEE HOPE
Author of The Blythe Girls Books

Every Volume Complete in Itself.

These are the adventures of a group of bright, fun-loving, up-to-date girls who have a common bond in their fondness for outdoor life, camping, travel and adventure. There is excitement and humor in these stories and girls will find in them the kind of pleasant associations that they seek to create among their own friends and chums.

GROSSET & DUNLAP, *Publishers,* **NEW YORK**

CAROLYN WELLS BOOKS

Attractively Bound. Illustrated. Colored Wrappers.

THE MARJORIE BOOKS

Marjorie is a happy little girl of twelve, up to mischief, but full of goodness and sincerity. In her and her friends every girl reader will see much of her own love of fun, play and adventure.

MARJORIE'S VACATION
MARJORIE'S BUSY DAYS
MARJORIE'S NEW FRIEND
MARJORIE IN COMMAND
MARJORIE'S MAYTIME
MARJORIE AT SEACOTE

THE TWO LITTLE WOMEN SERIES

Introducing Dorinda Fayre—a pretty blonde, sweet, serious, timid and a little slow, and Dorothy Rose—a sparkling brunette, quick, elf-like, high tempered, full of mischief and always getting into scrapes.

TWO LITTLE WOMEN
TWO LITTLE WOMEN AND TREASURE
HOUSE
TWO LITTLE WOMEN ON A HOLIDAY

THE DICK AND DOLLY BOOKS

Dick and Dolly are brother and sister, and their games, their pranks, their joys and sorrows, are told in a manner which makes the stories "really true" to young readers.

DICK AND DOLLY
DICK AND DOLLY'S ADVENTURES

GROSSET & DUNLAP, PUBLISHERS, NEW YORK

FLYING STORIES FOR BOYS

IN THE AIR WITH ANDY LANE
By EUSTACE L. ADAMS

Illustrated.   Every Volume Complete in Itself.

Mr. Adams, the author of this flying series for boys is an experienced aviator and has had many thrilling adventures in the air—both as a member of the famous Lafayette Escadrille in the World War and in the United States Naval Aviation Service flying with the squadrons patrolling the Atlantic Coast. His stories reveal not only his ability to tell daring and exciting air episodes but also his first hand knowledge of modern aeroplanes and the marvelous technical improvements which have been made in the past few years. Andy Lane flies the latest and most highly developd machines in the field of aviation.

FIFTEEN DAYS IN THE AIR
Andy refuels his ship in the air and sets a new endurance record.

OVER THE POLAR ICE
In a giant flying boat Andy beats his enemy in a dash to the South Pole.

RACING ROUND THE WORLD
In a series of thrilling flights Andy wins an air dash around the globe to win a $100,000 prize.

THE RUNAWAY AIRSHIP
Through foggy skies Andy Lane brings back the world's greatest passenger carrying dirigible, blown away on the wings of a storm.

PIRATES OF THE AIR
Andy Lane pilots the giant passenger plane Apex No. 4 across the Atlantic in the face of almost overwhelming odds.

ON THE WINGS OF FLAME
Andy makes a forced landing in the South American jungle in the dead of night and has thrilling experiences with the natives.

THE FLYING WINDMILL
Andy Lane and his restless crew take off in a monster autogyro in search of pirate treasure.

GROSSET & DUNLAP, Publishers, NEW YORK

WESTERN STORIES FOR BOYS

By JAMES CODY FERRIS

**Individual Colored Wrappers and Illustrations by
WALTER S. ROGERS
Each Volume Complete in Itself.**

Thrilling tales of the great west, told primarily for boys but which will be read by all who love mystery, rapid action, and adventures in the great open spaces.

The Manly Boys, Roy and Teddy, are the sons of an old ranchman, the owner of many thousands of heads of cattle. The lads know how to ride, how to shoot, and how to take care of themselves under any and all circumstances.

The cowboys of the X Bar X Ranch are real cowboys, on the job when required but full of fun and daring—a bunch any reader will be delighted to know.

THE X BAR X BOYS ON THE RANCH
THE X BAR X BOYS IN THUNDER CANYON
THE X BAR X BOYS ON WHIRLPOOL RIVER
THE X BAR X BOYS ON BIG BISON TRAIL
THE X BAR X BOYS AT THE ROUND-UP
THE X BAR X BOYS AT NUGGET CAMP
THE X BAR X BOYS AT RUSTLER'S GAP
THE X BAR X BOYS AT GRIZZLY PASS
THE X BAR X BOYS LOST IN THE ROCKIES

GROSSET & DUNLAP, PUBLISHERS, NEW YORK